DATE			

JANICE VANCLEAVE'S
SPECTACULAR SCIENCE PROJECTS

Animals
Earthquakes
Electricity
Gravity
Machines
Magnets
Microscopes and Magnifying Lenses
Molecules
Volcanoes

JANICE VANCLEAVE'S
SCIENCE FOR EVERY KID SERIES

Astronomy for Every Kid
Biology for Every Kid
Chemistry for Every Kid
Dinosaurs for Every Kid
Earth Science for Every Kid
Geography for Every Kid
Geometry for Every Kid
Human Body for Every Kid
Math for Every Kid
Physics for Every Kid

Spectacular Science Projects

JANICE VANCLEAVE'S
WEATHER

MIND-BOGGLING EXPERIMENTS YOU CAN TURN INTO SCIENCE FAIR PROJECTS

John Wiley & Sons, Inc.
New York • Chichester • Brisbane • Toronto • Singapore

This text is printed on acid-free paper.

Design and Production by Navta Associates, Inc.
Illustrated by Doris Ettlinger

Library of Congress Cataloging-in-Publication Data
VanCleave, Janice.
 [Weather]
 Janice VanCleave's weather: mind-boggling experiments you can turn into science fair projects / Janice VanCleave.
 p.   cm. – (Janice VanCleave's spectacular science projects) (Janice VanCleave's science for every kid series)
 Includes index.
 ISBN 0-471-03231-X
 1. Weather—Experiments—Juvenile literature. 2. Science—Experiments—Methodology—Juvenile literature. 3. Science exhibitions—Juvenile literature. 4. Science projects—Juvenile literature. [1. Weather—Experiments. 2. Experiments. 3. Science Projects.] I. Title. II. Title: Weather. III. Series: VanCleave, Janice Pratt. Janice VanCleave's spectacular science projects. IV. Series: VanCleave, Janice Pratt. Janice VanCleave's science for every kid series.
 QC981.3.V36   1995
 551,5'078–dc20   93-25646

Printed in the United States of America
10 9 8

CONTENTS

Introduction   1
  1. Straight On!   4
  2. Blue Sky   8
  3. Highs and Lows   12
  4. Up and Down   16
  5. More Heat   20
  6. Hot Box   24
  7. On the Move   28
  8. Windy   32
  9. Fronts   36
 10. Cloud Maker   40
 11. Rainy   44
 12. Dew Drops   48
 13. Frosty   52
 14. Icy   56
 15. Layered   60
 16. Flashers!   64
 17. Boom!   68
 18. Twister   72
 19. Stormy   76
 20. Indicators   80
Glossary   84
Index   88

I would like to dedicate this book to Terra Phillips and to the children in my granddaughter Lauren Russell's, class at Bear Branch Elementary School: Jessica Beuer, Anna Carriker, Rebekah Fontenot, Michael Garcia, Windy Hall, Michelle Haskin, Jessica Honsinger, Jonathan Hutcherson, Maureen Maloney, Cody McGee, Shannon Montgomery, Matthew Passmore, Timothy Peters, Patrick Pierson, Kaleb Pomeroy, Alexandra Rodriguez, Kent Rohrer, Lauren Russell, Anna Sanders, Joshua Sebree, Steven (Lewis) Small, Lacy Thomas, Nicole Zielenski.

A special note of thanks to Lauren's teacher, Ms. Kay Lester, and to her principal, Mr. Kyle Fontenot, for their part in encouraging Lauren and the other Bear Branch students to value science education.

Introduction

Science is a search for answers. Science projects are good ways to learn more about science as you search for the answers to specific problems. This book will give you guidance and provide ideas, but you must do your part in the search by planning experiments, finding and recording information related to the problem, and organizing the data collected to find the answer to the problem. Sharing your findings by presenting your project at science fairs will be a rewarding experience if you have properly prepared for the exhibit. Trying to assemble a project overnight results in frustration, and you cheat yourself out of the fun of being a science detective. Solving a scientific mystery, like solving a detective mystery, requires planning and the careful collecting of facts. The following sections provide suggestions for how to get started on this scientific quest. Start the project with curiosity and a desire to learn something new.

SELECT A TOPIC

The 20 topics in this book suggest many possible problems to solve. Each topic has one "cookbook" experiment—follow the recipe and the result is guaranteed. Approximate metric equivalents have been given after all English measurements. Try several or all of these easy experiments before choosing the topic you like best and want to know more about. Regardless of the problem you choose to solve, what you discover will make you more knowledgeable about weather.

KEEP A JOURNAL

Purchase a bound notebook in which you will write everything relating to the project. This is your journal. It will contain your original ideas as well as ideas you get from books or from people like teachers and scientists. It will include descriptions of your experiments as well as diagrams, photographs, and written observations of all your results. Every entry should be as neat as possible and dated. Information from this journal can be used to write a report of your project, and you will want to display the journal with your completed project. A neat, orderly journal provides a complete and accurate record of your project from start to finish. It is also proof of the time you spent sleuthing out the answers to the scientific mystery you undertook to solve.

LET'S EXPLORE

This section of each chapter follows each of 20 sample experiments and provides additional questions about the problem presented in the experiment. By making small changes to some part of the sample experiment, new results are achieved. Think about why these new results might have happened. **Caution:** Do not substitute chemicals in the experiment without approval of a knowledgeable person.

SHOW TIME!

You can use the format of the sample experiment to design your own experiments to solve the questions asked in "Let's Explore." Your own experiment should follow the sample experiment's format and include a single question about one idea, a list of necessary materials, a detailed step-by-step procedure, written results with diagrams, graphs, and charts if they seem helpful, and a conclusion answering and explaining the question. Include any information you found through research to clarify your answer. When you design your own experiments, make sure to get adult approval if supplies or procedures other than those given in this book are used.

If you want to make a science fair project, study the information listed here and after each sample experiment in the book to develop your ideas into a real science fair exhibit. Use the suggestions that best apply to the project topic that you have chosen. Keep in mind that while your display represents all the work that you have done, it must tell the story of the project in such a way that it attracts and holds the interest of the viewer. So keep it simple. Do not try to cram all of your information into one place. To have more space on the display and still exhibit all your work, keep some of the charts, graphs, pictures, and other materials in your journal instead of on the display board itself.

The actual size and shape of displays can be different, depending on the local science fair officials, so you will have to check the rules for your science fair. Most exhibits are allowed to be 48 inches (122 cm) wide, 30 inches (76 cm) deep, and 108 inches (274 cm) high. These are maximum measurements and your display may be smaller than this. A three-sided backboard (see drawing) is usually the best way to display your work. Wooden panels can be hinged together, but you can also use sturdy cardboard pieces taped together to form a very inexpensive but presentable exhibit.

A good title of six words or less with a maximum of 50 characters should be placed at the top of the center panel. The title should capture the theme of the project but should not be the same as the problem statement. For example, if the problem under question is *Where are tornadoes most likely to occur?*, a good title of the project may be "Tornado Alley." The title and other headings should be neat and large enough to be readable at a distance of about 3 feet (1 meter). You can glue letters to the backboard (you can use precut letters that you buy or letters that you cut out of construction paper), or you can stencil the letters for all the titles. A short summary paragraph of about 100 words to explain the scientific principles involved is good and can be printed under the title. A person who has no knowledge of the topic should be able to easily understand the basic idea of the project just from reading the summary. Allow friends and adults to read the summary and ask for their reactions. Did they understand your project? It is up to you to clarify any items that need explaining.

There are no set rules about the position of the information on the display. However, it all needs to be well organized, with the title and summary paragraph as the main point at the top of the center and the remaining material placed neatly from left to right under specific headings. Choices of headings will depend on how you wish to display the information. Separate headings for Problem, Procedure, Results, and Conclusion may be used.

The judges give points for how clearly you are able to discuss the project and explain its purpose, procedure, results, and conclusion. The display should be organized so that it explains everything, but your ability to discuss your project and answer the questions of the judges convinces them that you did the work and understand what you have done. Practice a speech in front of friends, and invite them to ask you questions. If you do not know the answer to a question, never guess or make up an answer or just say, "I do not know." Instead, you can say that you did not discover that answer during your research and then offer other information that you found of interest about the project. Be proud of the project and approach the judges with enthusiasm about your work.

CHECK IT OUT!

Read about your topic in many books and magazines. You are more likely to have a successful project if you are well informed about the topic. For the topics in this book, some tips are provided about specific places to look for information. Record in your journal all the information you find, and include for each source the author's name, the book title (or magazine name and article title), the numbers of the pages you read, the publisher's name, where it was published, and the year of publication.

Straight On!

PROBLEM

How does the curved shape of the earth affect the climate throughout the world?

Materials

sheet of typing paper
modeling clay
two new, unsharpened pencils
pen

Procedure

1. Turn the paper sideways on a table.

2. Mold a walnut-sized piece of clay into a 1½-inch (3.75-cm) column.

3. Place the clay on the top left edge of the paper.

4. Lay the eraser of one pencil on top of the clay column so that the end of the pencil rests on the paper.

5. Hold the second pencil on top of the first one and slide it downward along the top of the first pencil until its tip just touches the paper, as shown in the diagram.

6. Use the pen to mark where each pencil touches the paper.

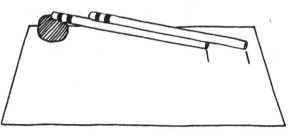

7. Move the two pencils to a vertical position so that they stand side by side on the paper.

8. Use the pen to mark where the left side of each pencil touches the paper.

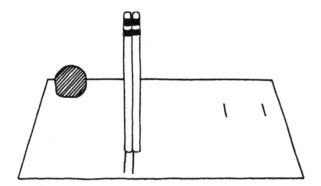

9. Compare the distance between the first two marks to the distance between the second two marks.

Results

The marks made when the pencils were slanted are farther apart than the marks made when the pencils were in a vertical position.

Why?

Variations in **weather** are caused by changing conditions throughout the **atmosphere** (blanket of gases known as air surrounding the earth), including changes in temperature, pressure, **humidity** (amount of water vapor in the air), wind, and **precipitation** (liquid or solid particles that form in the atmosphere and then fall to the earth's surface). The heat of the sun warms the earth and its atmosphere. Because the earth is curved, some regions and materials heat up more quickly than others, creating warmer air masses and cooler air masses. The movement of these air masses causes changes in weather. Thus, the sun's energy is the fuel that keeps the atmosphere in a state of constant change.

The sun's rays hit different regions of the earth at different angles, creating distinct **climates** (average weather over long periods of time) throughout the world. Generally, the hottest places on earth are near the **equator** (the imaginary line around the center of the earth), which receive the most direct rays from the sun (the areas from A to B in the diagram). Places farther from the equator

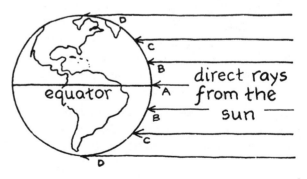

tend to be cooler because the sun's rays strike the ground there at an angle. The same amount of sunlight is spread over a larger area in other places on the earth (B to C and C to D in the diagram).

The pencils in this experiment represent the sun's rays. The vertical pencils are direct rays received at the equator, and the slanted pencils are angled rays received near the **north and south poles** (areas farthest north and south, respectively, from the equator). The marks on the paper indicate the areas heated by the rays. The slanted rays mark off a wider area. Places that receive slanted rays from the sun are cooler because the same amount of heat is spread over a larger area.

LET'S EXPLORE

Repeat the original experiment twice, changing the height of the clay first to 3 inches (7.5 cm) and then to 5 inches (12.5 cm). **Science Fair Hint:** Take photographs with the pencils being held at different angles against a map of the earth. These photos can be used as part of a project display to represent how the sun's rays strike the earth at different angles in different locations between the earth's equator and its poles.

SHOW TIME!

1a. Demonstrate the effect the tilt of the earth has on the amount of sunlight the earth receives during the different **seasons** (four periods of the year, each with specific weather conditions, called spring, summer, autumn, and winter). Insert a pencil through a ball of clay. Use a second pencil to mark the equator line around the center of the clay ball. Position the ball on a table so that the pencil eraser is leaning slightly to the right. In a darkened room, shine a flashlight about 6 inches (15 cm) from the left side of the ball and observe where the light strikes the ball. Move the light to the right side of the ball and observe where the light strikes the ball again. The part that receives the most light represents the warmest area on the earth. Determine what position the earth is in when the weather is at its warmest where you live. Photographs can be used to represent the procedure and the results of this experiment.

b. Find out more about the position of the earth during each of the four seasons. Prepare and display diagrams showing the earth's position during the different seasons where you live.

CHECK IT OUT!

The earth is divided into distinct climate regions. Find out more about these regions. What are their names? How many regions are there? What type of weather occurs in each region? Create and display a map of the earth showing the different regions. Information related to this project can be found on pages 167–175 of *Janice VanCleave's Geography for Every Kid* (New York: Wiley, 1993).

2

Blue Sky

PROBLEM

How do particles in the atmosphere cause the sky to look blue and the sun to look yellow?

Materials

masking tape
sheet of typing paper
box with sides at least 8½ × 11 inches
    (21.3 cm × 27.5 cm)
7-ounce (210-ml) clear plastic glass
tap water
flashlight
eyedropper
thick, milky, dishwashing liquid
spoon

Procedure

1. Tape the typing paper to the inside bottom of the box.

2. Set the box on its side on a table.

3. Fill the glass three-fourths full with water.

4. Set the glass inside the box near the front edge.

5. Darken the room and use the flashlight to direct a light beam through the center of the glass.

6. Observe the color of the light on the white paper behind the glass and the color of the water in the glass.

7. Add one drop of dishwashing liquid to the water and stir.

8. Again, place the glass inside the box and shine the light beam through the center of the glass.

9. Observe the color of the light on the white paper behind the glass and the color of the soapy water in the glass.

Results

Light passing through the water produces a white spot of light on the paper and makes the water look bright, but it has no color. Light passing through the soapy water produces a yellow spot on the paper and gives the water a bluish appearance.

Why?

Light is a form of energy that travels in waves like water waves. The color of light depends on its **wavelength** (distance from the top of one wave to the top of the next wave). The order of the seven colors of the rainbow are red, orange, yellow, green, blue, indigo, and violet. These colors are called the **visible spectrum** and are in order from the longest to the shortest wavelength, red being the longest and violet the shortest.

Light from the flashlight, like light from the sun, looks white, but is actually a combination of all the rainbow colors. When the light waves from the flashlight pass through the soapy water, they come in contact with small soap particles and the shorter blue wavelengths of light and are scattered in different directions. You see more blue light, so the soapy water looks blue.

This same kind of scattering of blue light waves occurs as sunlight passes through the atmosphere, the blanket of air surrounding the earth. Air **molecules** (the smallest unit of substance that still is that substance) in the atmosphere are just the right size to scatter the shorter wavelengths of light, mostly the blue light rays. No matter which direction you look, blue light waves from the sky come to your eyes. This is what makes the sky look blue. The combination of the remaining light waves produces a yellow color. This is what causes the yellow spot on the paper and also causes the sun to appear yellow.

LET'S EXPLORE

1. At sunset and sunrise the sun is farther away from you than when it is

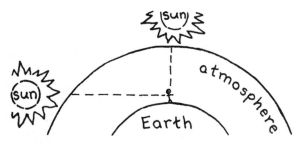

directly overhead. During this time, the sunlight has to pass through more of the atmosphere to reach you. This longer journey through the air means more of the shorter waves of light are scattered. Few reach your eye. The longer wavelengths of yellow, orange, and red light waves are scattered less, so you see more of these colors causing you to see a flaming sky. Demonstrate this effect by increasing the number of soap particles in the water. Repeat the original experiment, adding one drop of dishwashing liquid at a time until 15 drops have been added. Compare the colors of the light that appear on the paper after each drop of soap is added.

Science Fair Hint: Find out how the sky's color can be used as a weather predictor. How accurate are weather proverbs such as: "Red sky in the morning, sailors take warning; red sky at night, sailors' delight"? Display this and other weather proverbs. Include information about the accuracy of their predictions. One source for this information is on pages 53–56 of *The Weather Companion* by Gary Lockhart (New York: Wiley, 1979).

SHOW TIME!

Sunlight travels about 93 million miles through space to reach the outer edges of the earth's atmosphere. The earth's atmosphere is divided into layers. Starting with the outer layer, their names are exosphere, ionosphere, mesophere, stratosphere, and troposphere. Find out more about the earth's atmosphere and draw a diagram of the earth and its atmospheric layers.

Each atmospheric layer differs from the others in distance from the earth, presence of air, temperature, color, and what occurs in it. On one side of the diagram, indicate where each layer begins and the distance from its starting point to the earth. While the diagram will show a specific starting point for each layer, remember that there is no real barrier dividing each layer. Label the temperature of each layer on the other side of the diagram. Find out about air composition and events that occur in each layer. Which layer is responsible for the earth's weather? Add drawings and labels to the diagram showing such things as the location of clouds, the aurora borealis, the path of the Concord, the jet stream, and where meteors burn up.

CHECK IT OUT!

Sunlight contains more than just colored light waves. Some of the waves are high-energy waves called *ultraviolet light waves*, which can destroy living cells and tissue. Find out more about ultraviolet (UV) light. How is it involved in the production of the ozone layer? How does the ozone layer prevent UV rays from reaching the earth? How does the ozone layer affect the temperature of the earth's atmosphere and surface?

3

Highs and Lows

PROBLEM

How can low air pressure be determined?

Materials

16-ounce (480-ml) glass soda bottle
tap water
ruler
red food coloring
drinking straw
scissors
modeling clay
marking pen
helper

Procedure

1. Make a barometer by following these instructions:

- Fill the bottle with tap water to about 1 inch (2.5 cm) below its top.

- Add enough food coloring to make the water a dark red. Swirl the bottle to thoroughly mix the water and coloring.

- At a point 2 inches (5 cm) from one end of the straw cut three-fourths of the way through the straw with the scissors. Bend the short end over.

- Insert about 3 inches (7.5 cm) of the straw into the soda bottle with the bent end up.

- Mold a piece of clay around the straw and seal the mouth of the bottle.

- Press down on the clay until the water rises to about a half inch (1.25 cm) below the cut in the straw.

- With the pen, mark the top of the water level in the straw.

2. Ask your helper to hold the bent end of the straw at a right angle to the rest of the straw, and blow hard through the bent end.

3. Observe the height of the water in the straw as your helper blows through the straw.

Results

The water level in the straw rises.

Why?

Air is a mixture of different gas molecules that, like all gas molecules, move around at very fast speeds. They bump into each other and anything else that crosses their path, and these collisions create pressure called air pressure or **atmospheric pressure** (force caused by the impact of moving air molecules on an area of the earth or any other object). Air pressure depends on the number of air molecules in a specific area and how fast they move. An increase in the number and/or speed of the molecules causes an increase in pressure.

The **barometer** (an instrument used to measure air pressure) made in this experiment can be used to detect changes in air pressure. Air inside the bottle pushes down on the surface of the water with a constant amount of pressure. At the same time, air pushes down on the water inside the straw. When you blow across the straw, the moving stream of air reduces the pressure on the water inside the straw. The change in pressure means that the air pressure inside the bottle is greater than the air pressure inside the straw, so the water is pushed up the straw.

LET'S EXPLORE

1. How would a slower stream of air across the top of the straw affect the results? Repeat the experiment, blowing very gently through the horizontal straw.

2. How would an increase in air pressure affect the results? Repeat the original experiment, raising the bent end and

blowing air directly into the straw in the bottle.

SHOW TIME!

1. Use the bottle barometer made in the original experiment to observe changes in air pressure over a period of one or more weeks. Place a drop of oil on top of the straw to prevent the water from evaporating. Prepare a scale by using a fine-tip pen to mark millimeter lines on a piece of tape 2 inches (5 cm) long. Start at the top of the straw and stick the marked tape down the side. Observe and record the height of water in the straw every day. A record of the general type of weather each day, such as cold, warm, rainy, or dry, can also be made. Use your records to determine if and how air pressure affects the weather.

2. Another barometer can be constructed by cutting the bottom off a 9-inch (23-cm) balloon, as shown in the diagram.

Stretch the bottom section of the balloon over the mouth of the small jar. Secure the balloon section to the jar with a rubber band. Glue the large end of a flat toothpick to the balloon section. Allow the glue to dry before placing the jar inside a wide-mouth, quart (liter) jar.

Stretch the top section of the cut balloon over the mouth of the large jar. Again, secure the balloon to the jar with a rubber band. Tie a knot in the neck of the balloon.

Test the effects of decreased pressure by pulling up on the knot. Test the effects of increased pressure by pushing down on the knot. For each test, observe the position of the end of the toothpick on the small jar.

top

bottom

CHECK IT OUT!

The barometer was invented by Evangelista Torricelli (1609-1647), an Italian mathematician and physicist. Torricelli used mercury in his barometer. The mercury barometers used today are very similar to the one invented by Torricelli. How does the mercury barometer work? Describe Torricelli's technique in constructing his mercury barometer. Is this same technique used today? Why?

4

Up and Down

PROBLEM

How can you make a model of a Fahrenheit thermometer?

Materials

two sheets of white poster board, each 22 × 28 inches (55 × 70 cm)
yardstick (meterstick)
scissors
red crayon
marking pen
transparent tape

Procedure

1. From one of the sheets of poster board, cut a 14-by-28-inch (35-by-70-cm) strip and an 8-by-28-inch (20-by-70-cm) strip.

2. Color the bulb on the large strip and one side of the narrower strip red.

3. On the larger strip, draw a thermome-

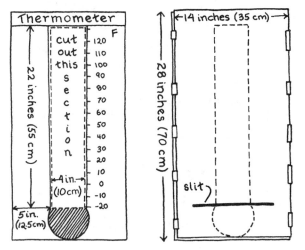

ter using the measurements shown in the diagram.

4. Cut out and remove the 4-by-22-inch (10-by-55-cm) section above the thermometer bulb.

5. From the second sheet of poster board, cut a 14-by-28-inch (35-by-70-cm) strip.

6. Cut a 10-inch (25-cm) slit 4 inches (10 cm) from the short edge of the strip. The slit should be centered horizontally.

7. Place the strip behind the thermometer and tape the edges of the two strips together.

8. Insert the narrow paper strip into the slit so that the red side shows through the cut-out section of the thermometer.

9. Holding the poster, slowly pull the red strip down and observe its height at each temperature mark.

Results

Moving the red-colored strip up and down makes the temperature reading on the thermometer increase and decrease.

Why?

A **thermometer** is an instrument used to measure temperature. **Temperature** measures how hot a material is, which equals the average **kinetic energy** (energy of motion) of the molecules in the material. The higher the temperature of a material, the faster its molecules are moving around. As molecules move faster, they move farther apart. In a real thermometer, as the material in the bulb gets hotter, it expands and moves up the tube. As the material cools, its molecules move slower and move closer together, and the material moves down the thermometer tube.

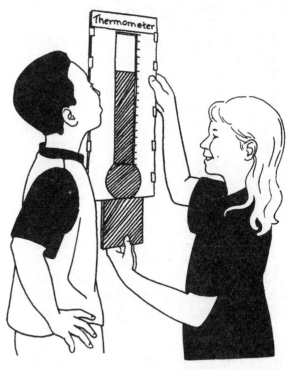

A thermometer is **calibrated**. This means that the different heights along the tube are marked so that the distance from one mark to the next represents a change of the same number of degrees in the temperature of the material.

LET'S EXPLORE

1. Use a thermometer calibrated in both Fahrenheit and Celsius to mark Celsius degrees on the model. **Science Fair Hint:** Find out more about the thermometer scales of Fahrenheit and Celsius and how they differ. Display examples of calculations showing how Fahrenheit degrees are mathematically changed to Celsius degrees and examples of Celsius degrees changed to Fahrenheit degrees.

2. Weather is the result of changing conditions in the blanket of air surrounding the earth called the atmosphere. The study of weather is called **meteorology**, and the scientists who study weather are called **meteorologists**. One condition of the atmosphere that changes is its temperature.

Meteorologists often refer to the freezing point of water (32 degrees Fahrenheit and 0 degrees Celsius) when measuring air temperature. A temperature expected to be below freezing indicates that the air temperature will drop below 32 degrees Fahrenheit (0 degrees Celsius). Mark the freezing point of water on the thermometer model. **Science Fair Hint:** Display the model as part of your project.

SHOW TIME!

1. Another way to demonstrate how a thermometer works is by constructing a bottle thermometer. Stand a very thin straw in a cup half filled with water that has been tinted with blue food coloring. While the straw is in the water, place your index finger over the open end of the straw. Keeping your finger over the straw, lift the straw out of the colored water and insert the free end into an empty soda bottle. Ask a helper to seal the mouth of the bottle by wrapping clay around the straw; then remove your finger from over the end of the straw. Fill a

bowl with warm tap water. Fill a second bowl with cold tap water and add two or three ice cubes. Place the soda bottle containing the straw in the warm water. When the colored water in the straw starts to rise, remove the bottle from the water and quickly set it in the bowl of ice water. Display drawings that show the position of the colored water in the straw when the bottle thermometer is heated and cooled.

warm water

ice cube

ice water

2. Your skin can sense changes in temperature. See if your skin can give you accurate information about temperature. Number three bowls and fill them with water of different temperatures: Bowl 1, lukewarm; Bowl 2, cool; Bowl 3, icy cold. Ask a helper to place a finger in Bowl 1 and a second helper to place a finger in Bowl 3. After 30 seconds, instruct both helpers to immediately place their fingers in Bowl 2. Have them each describe the temperature of the water in Bowl 2.

CHECK IT OUT!

A weather observer could not give a complete report of weather conditions without knowing the air temperature. The thermometer is thus a tool that is very important to meteorology. Find out more about the thermometer. Who invented the first thermometer? Who suggested the first thermometer scale? What kinds of thermometers did Gabriel D. Fahrenheit, Anders Celsius, and Lord Kelvin introduce? Information about thermometers can be found on pages 181–187 in *Janice VanCleave's A+ Projects In Chemistry* (New York: Wiley, 1993).

More Heat

PROBLEM

Which warms faster, water or soil?

Materials

small box with measurements at least
     10 × 10 × 10 inches (25 × 25 × 25 cm)
two 7-ounce (21-ml) paper cups
light-colored soil
tap water
two thermometers
ruler
duct tape
paper
pencil
timer
desk lamp
adult helper

Procedure

1. Ask an adult to cut the top off and cut out one side of the box.
2. Fill one cup with soil and the other with water.
3. Place the cups together at the back of the box.
4. Put a thermometer in each cup. The bulb of each thermometer should be about one-fourth inch (0.64 cm) below the surface of the water or the soil in the cup.
5. Tape the top of each thermometer to the back of the box.
6. Prepare a chart to record the experimental results.

Temperature Changes

Materials	Temperature		
	Starting	Final	Change
light-colored soil			
tap water			

7. After the thermometers have been in the cups for at least 5 minutes, record the temperature of each material. These are the starting temperatures.

8. Place the box under the lamp so that the light bulb is about 10 inches (25 cm) from the top of the cups. Make sure that the light bulb does not touch the box.

9. After 10 minutes, turn the lamp off and immediately record the temperature in each cup. These are the final temperatures.

10. Calculate and record the changes between the starting temperatures and the final temperatures.

Results

The temperature of the soil has increased more than has the temperature of the water.

Why?

Heat is the total energy of all particles in an object. When heat energy from the light is added to the object, its total energy increases. While the addition of heat usually causes the temperature of the object to increase, the same amount of heat does not cause the same change in temperature in all substances. The amount of heat needed to raise the temperature of one pound of substance one degree Fahrenheit (one gram of substance one degree Celsius) is called **specific heat**.

Although the same amount of heat is added to both cups, the temperature change is not the same for the two materials. Water does not heat up as quickly as soil does; thus water has a higher specific heat than does the soil. This experiment indicates that the earth's land surfaces with the type of soil used in the experiment heat up more rapidly than do its water surfaces.

LET'S EXPLORE

1. Do the materials cool at the same rate? Repeat the experiment, but record the temperatures as soon as the lamp has been turned off as the starting temperature. After the lamp has been off for 10 minutes, record the temperatures as the final temperatures. Calculate the temperature change for each cup.

Science Fair Hint: Prepare bar graphs similar to the one shown here to display the results of heating and cooling the soil and water. Number the temperature divisions on your graph, using either the Fahrenheit or Celsius scale.

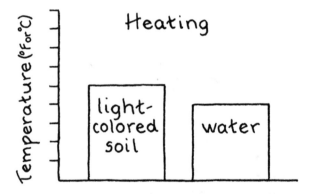

2. Does the color of the material affect the amount of heat needed to change its temperature? Repeat the original experiment using soils of different

colors. You may want to collect soil samples from different locations during a vacation or ask friends to send you soil. Use red, black, and other colors of soil. **Science Fair Hint:** Use a bar graph to compare the results of the different soils.

SHOW TIME!

1. Is the temperature of the air above the materials affected when the materials are heated? Fill two 7-ounce (21-ml) paper cups half full, one with water and the other with dark-colored soil. Place the cups in the opened box. Hold a thermometer in each cup with the bulb just above the surface of the material, and secure it to the box with tape. After 5 minutes, record the temperature of the air. Remove the thermometers and heat the cups under a lamp for 10 minutes as in the original experiment. Wait one minute; then, place a thermometer in each cup as before. Wait another minute; then

record the air temperature above the heated materials.

2. Do structures affect the earth's surface temperature? Read and record the temperatures on two thermometers. Place one thermometer on the ground (on either grass or pavement) in the shade of a tree, building, or other large structure. Place the second thermometer on the same type of surface, but in direct sunlight. Record the temperature on both thermometers every 5 minutes for 30 minutes. Use graphs to display the results.

CHECK IT OUT!

The difference in the rates at which the earth's land and water surfaces heat and cool causes differences in surface temperatures. Find out how different surface temperatures affect weather. How does surface temperature affect air temperature? What effect does air temperature have on wind production?

6

Hot Box

PROBLEM

What is the greenhouse effect?

Materials

shoebox
soil
two thermometers
colorless plastic food wrap
timer

Procedure

1. Half fill the shoebox with soil.

2. Lay one of the thermometers on the surface of the soil. Keep the second thermometer outside of the box.

3. Cover the opening of the box with a single layer of plastic wrap.

4. Take a reading from both thermometers.

5. Place the box and second thermometer side by side in a sunny place outdoors.

6. Record readings from both thermometers every 15 minutes for one hour.

7. Record readings every hour thereafter for four hours.

Results

All or most all of the temperature readings show that the temperature inside the plastic-covered box was higher than the temperature outside the box.

Why?

A structure designed to provide a protected, controlled environment for raising plants indoors is called a **greenhouse**. It is made of glass or other material that allows the sun's light to pass through. The box in this experiment is an example of a greenhouse.

Solar radiation, the energy that is emitted by the sun, comes in the form of energy waves of varying wavelengths.

The short-wavelength radiation from the sun passes freely through the plastic wrap covering the box. Most of these rays are taken in by the soil and cardboard sides of the box, causing them to heat up. Long-wavelength radiation, called **infrared waves** (heat rays), are then released by the soil and the cardboard sides.

Some scientists think that the material that makes up a greenhouse allows short-wavelength radiation to pass through but blocks the escape of long-wavelength radiation. In other words, short-wavelength radiation enters the box through the plastic and changes into long-wavelength radiation, or heat waves, which are then trapped inside by the plastic. Other scientists believe that because greenhouses are closed, heated air becomes trapped inside. Since no cooling air can enter the box, the temperature inside the greenhouse increases.

The earth's atmosphere, however, does trap the long-wavelength radiation. **Atmospheric gases** are the gases that make up the layer of air surrounding the earth. The composition of gases in air is about 78 percent nitrogen, 21 percent oxygen, and 1 percent water vapor, carbon dioxide, and other gases such as neon, sulfur dioxide, and carbon monoxide. Like the plastic over the box in the experiment, the atmosphere allows some of the sun's rays to pass through to the earth's surface. The surface heats up and gives off long-wavelength radiation. Most of these heat rays are absorbed by **water vapor** (water in its gas phase) and **carbon dioxide** (gas produced by burning fuels and exhaled by animals) in the lower atmosphere. These atmospheric gases reemit a large portion of the heat rays back toward the earth, which causes the earth's surface to gradually become warmer. The greenhouse and the atmosphere both trap warmth from the sun. For this reason, this warming of the earth is called the **greenhouse effect**.

LET'S EXPLORE

1. Does the type of cover on the box affect the results? Repeat the original experiment, preparing boxes with different covers. One can be covered with glass. Ask an adult to remove a piece of glass from a picture frame and to place masking tape around the edges. Cover other boxes with transparent plastic report folders of various colors. **Science Fair Hint:** Display samples of the box covers with the results of the experiment.

2. Do surface structures affect the results? Repeat the original experiment, preparing several boxes. Cover the surface of the soil in the boxes with different materials, such as rocks, leaves, and grass. **Science Fair Hint:** Display photographs of the various boxes with the results of the experiment.

3. Design ways to cover the box so that you can determine if it is the lack of air circulation or the trapped heat rays that affect the temperature change.

SHOW TIME!

1. The gases in the earth's atmosphere keep the earth from cooling too quickly at night. Simulate the atmosphere's effect on temperature by preparing two boxes as in the original experiment, but leave one box uncovered. Put the boxes outdoors in a sunny area for three hours, and then place

them inside the house in a dark area such as a closet. Read the thermometers every 15 minutes for one hour and then every 30 minutes for at least two hours thereafter.

2. **Ozone** is a form of oxygen that contains three combined oxygen atoms; the oxygen we breathe contains two combined oxygen atoms. The largest amount of ozone exists at a height between 10 and 20 miles (16 and 32 km) above the earth's surface; this area of the atmosphere is called the **ozone layer**. Some scientists think that reduction of the ozone layer would allow more radiation from the sun to reach the earth's surface, eventually causing climate changes. **Terrariums** (closed containers housing small plants and possibly some small animals such as snails, frogs, or snakes) can be used to simulate, though not exactly, the effect of increased solar radiation. Prepare two small, identical terrariums using instructions from a nursery or a book

on building terrariums. Insert a thermometer in each terrarium. Place one terrarium near a window where it will receive direct sunlight most of the day. Place the other terrarium away from direct sunlight, but in a lighted area. Observe both terrariums for at least 30 days. Take photos of the terrariums at the beginning and then on random days during the experiment. Find out more about the ozone layer and how people are causing it to change. Use this information to prepare a poster and display it along with the terrariums.

7

On the Move

PROBLEM

What causes wind?

Materials

ruler
scissors
tissue paper
paper hole-punch
thread
tape
new, unsharpened pencil

Procedure

1. Make a wind detector by following these steps:
- Measure and cut a 1-by-3-inch (1.25-by-7.5-cm) strip of tissue paper.
- Use the hole-punch to make a hole in one end of the paper strip.
- Cut a 2-inch (5-cm) piece of thread.
- Tie one end of the thread through the hole in the paper strip.
- Use a small piece of tape to attach the free end of the thread to the pencil about 2 inches (5 cm) from the pencil's end.

2. Open an outside door about 2 inches (5 cm). Hold the wind detector at the bottom of the opening in the door.

3. Observe the direction of any movement in the hanging paper piece.

Results

Diagram A shows the paper strip blowing in toward the room. This is the

winter

A

summer

B

correct result during the winter. Diagram B shows the reverse movement of the paper that would occur during the summer if the room were air-conditioned.

Why?

Warm air molecules have more energy and move around faster than do less energetic cold-air molecules. The speedy warm-air molecules tend to move away from each other. So warm air, with its molecules spaced farther apart, is lighter than cold air, with its sluggish molecules huddled closer together. This causes warmer, lighter air to rise, and colder, heavier air to sink. This up and down movement of air due to differences in temperature is called **convection currents**.

Vertical movements of air, or any fluid, are called **currents**. The movements of air in general horizontal directions are called **winds**. Wind depends on differences in atmospheric pressure. High pressure is associated with cold air, and low pressure with warm air. As warmer, lighter air in low pressure areas rises, the cooler, heavier surface air moves in to take the place of the rising currents of warm air. Thus, winds move from high pressure areas to low pressure areas.

When the door is opened during the winter, cold air rushes into the bottom of the room and replaces the rising warm air. In the summer, however, the air-conditioned room is colder than the warm air outside. When the door is opened, the cold air from the bottom of the room rushes out. The paper on the wind detector used in this experiment is pushed in the direction in which the wind is blowing.

LET'S EXPLORE

1a. Would holding the wind detector at different heights affect the results? Repeat the experiment holding the detector at the top and then at the middle of the opening in the door.

b. You do not have to wait until next winter or summer to see what the results would be in that particular season. To test the results during the opposite season, repeat the original and previous experiments while standing on the outside of the door.

SHOW TIME!

1a. A refrigerator can be used to test the movement of warm and cold air. Open the refrigerator door about 8 inches (20 cm). Hold the wind detector at the bottom of the refrigerator just inside the door opening.

b. Test the flow of air at the top of the open refrigerator door. Close the door and then open it again. Hold the tester inside the door at the top of the refrigerator.

2a. Air currents move around the earth as the warm air near the equator rises and flows up toward the poles. The cold polar air sinks and flows down toward the equator. Simulate the movement of air currents due to convection by filling a small jar with warm water mixed with food coloring. Cover the mouth of the jar with aluminum foil and secure it with a rubber band. Stand the small jar inside a quart (liter) jar filled with cold clear water. Use a pencil point to make two small holes in the foil.

colored water

Use photographs of the results along with diagrams of the movement of winds around the earth found in earth science texts to prepare a poster showing wind movement due to differences in pressure.

b. A **convection cell** is a pattern of air circulation caused by the unequal heating of the earth's surface. Use an earth science text to find out more about convection cells. Prepare and display a diagram showing zones of rising and sinking air, updraft and downdraft regions, and the direction of air between the areas of different pressure.

CHECK IT OUT!

1. A *cyclone* is a rotating wind system with low pressure at the center. Find out more about cyclones. What causes the winds in a cyclone to rotate? How do anticyclones and cyclones differ? In what direction do the winds in a cyclone spin in the Northern Hemisphere? Southern Hemisphere?

2. The major wind systems around the earth are called *prevailing winds*. Find out more about prevailing winds. What factors determine the direction of prevailing winds? Where are the northeast and southeast trade winds? Why are they called trade winds? Where are the prevailing westerlies? What is the Coriolis effect? A diagram of the earth showing the prevailing winds can be displayed.

8

Windy

PROBLEM

How can the speed of wind be measured?

Materials

drawing compass
poster board square, 6 × 6 inches
   (15 cm × 15 cm)
scissors
ruler
marking pen
transparent tape
12-inch (30-cm) piece of thread
Ping-Pong ball

Procedure

1. Use the compass to draw a curved line connecting two diagonal corners of the piece of poster board as shown in the diagram.

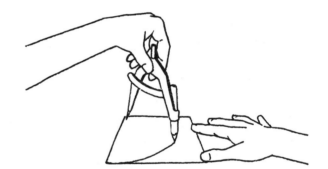

2. Cut along the curved line and keep the cone-shaped piece of paper. Discard the rest.

3. Lay the paper on a table with one straight edge at the top and the other straight edge to the right.

4. Prepare a scale on the curved edge of the paper by using the ruler and pen to make nine evenly spaced sections along the curved edge. Number them, starting with zero, as shown in the diagram.

5. Draw an arrow along the top edge pointing toward the corner of the paper.

6. Turn the ruler over and tape the paper to the top edge of the ruler as shown.

7. Tape one end of the thread to the Ping-Pong ball.

8. Tape the other end of the thread near the corner of the paper. The thread should hang so that it crosses the zero mark on the paper.

9. Stand outside in a windy area. Hold the ruler and point the arrow in the direction from which the wind is blowing.

10. Observe where the string crosses the paper scale.

Results

In a gentle breeze, the string moves slightly from its vertical position. A faster breeze causes the string to move farther up the scale.

Why?

The instrument you built is called an **anemometer**. An anemometer is used to measure how fast the wind blows. Moving air hits the Ping-Pong ball and causes it to move. The speed of the wind hitting the ball is indicated by the scale number to which the ball moves, as determined by the position of the string across the paper scale. The higher the number, the faster the wind is blowing.

LET'S EXPLORE

Use the anemometer you just made to measure the wind speed each day for a week or more. Record your readings in a data chart. **Science Fair Hint:** Use the information from the data chart to construct a graph similar to the graph shown here. Display the chart, graph, and anemometer as part of a project display.

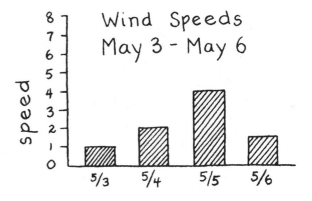

SHOW TIME!

1. Construct another type of anemometer called a Robinson anemometer by crossing two drinking straws and taping them together in the center where they cross. Use a pencil to punch a hole in the side of a 3-ounce (90-ml) paper cup near its rim. Do the same to three other cups that size. Place a cup on the end of each straw and secure with tape. All of the cups must face in the same direction. Ask an adult to stick a straight pin through the center of the straws and into the eraser of a pencil. Move the straws back and forth to enlarge the hole made by the pin so that the straws rotate easily

around the pin. Hold the pencil upright and position the cups about 12 inches (30 cm) from your face. Blow toward the open end of the cups to make sure the cups will spin around in a breeze. Use the cups to make comparisons of wind speeds on different days. The speed of the wind hitting the cups is determined by the number of turns per minute made by the cups. The faster the wind, the more turns per minute. Use this anemometer to determine wind speed (number of turns per minute) over several days. Compare your results with predicted wind speed from daily

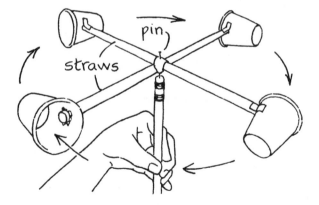

weather reports in the newspaper and/or local television. Display the anemometer and the collected results.

2. You can figure out the wind's direction simply by observing which way tree limbs, shrubs, or grass are blowing and then using a compass to determine what direction that is.

3. A **weather vane** (instrument that shows wind direction) can be constructed by marking the directions, N, NE, E, SE, S, SW, W, and NW along the rim of a paper plate. Place the plate on the ground in an unobstructed area. Attach a 4-inch (10-cm) piece of string to the top of a pencil eraser with a piece of tape. Insert the point of the pencil through the center of the paper plate and about 1 inch (2.5 cm) into the ground. Use a compass to determine which way is north, and rotate the paper plate until the N marked on the plate points north. The string will blow in the same direction as the wind. Photographs of the weather vane can be displayed.

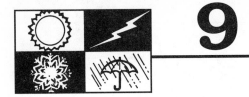

9

Fronts

PROBLEM

What are fronts?

Materials

9-inch (22.5-cm) glass pie plate
modeling clay
1 cup (250 ml) tap water
blue or any dark food coloring
spoon
1 cup (250 ml) liquid cooking oil
timer
helper

Procedure

1. Set the pie plate next to the edge of a table.

2. Use modeling clay to form a barrier across the center of the pie plate, dividing it into two equal parts.

3. Pour the water into the left side of the pie plate.

4. Add three drops of food coloring to the water and stir.

5. Pour the oil into the right side of the pie plate.

6. Kneel on the floor in front of the plate so that you are eye level with the plate.

7. Ask a helper to raise and remove the clay barrier from the plate.

8. Observe the movement of the two liquids for one to two minutes.

9. Look at the liquids as often as possible for 5 minutes or until no changes are seen.

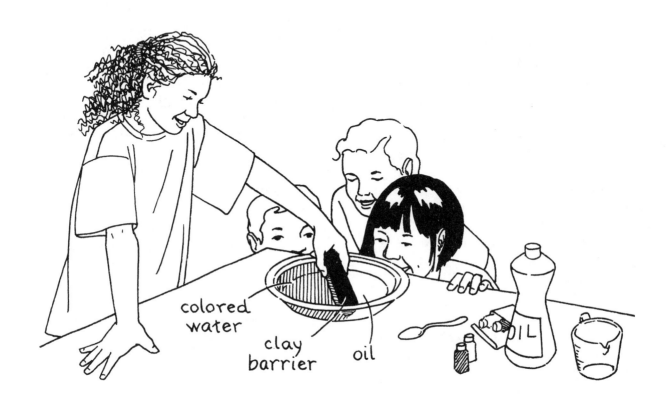

colored
water

clay
barrier

oil

Results

The colored water slowly moves under the layer of oil.

Why?

The **density** ("heaviness" of materials; mass compared to volume) of **air mass-** es (large bodies of air, each with about the same temperature and humidity throughout) varies in that different air masses have different temperatures and humidities. Cold air masses are more dense than warm air masses. Since water is more dense than oil, the colored water in the experiment represents a cold air mass and the oil represents a warm air mass. Just like the oil and water, cold and warm air masses do not mix with each other. The colder, more dense air mass generally moves under and lifts the warmer, less dense air mass.

The boundary between two air masses is called a **front**. The leading edge of a cold air mass advancing into an area occupied by warmer air is called a **cold front**. A **warm front** is the leading edge of a warm air mass moving into an area occupied by colder air. The weather is usually unsettled and stormy at a front. Precipitation is common, especially on the cold air side.

LET'S EXPLORE

Does the amount of each liquid affect the results? Repeat the experiment twice, first using one-half the amount of water, then using one-half the amount of oil. The results indicate whether the density of an air mass depends on its size.

SHOW TIME!

1. Generally a cold front wedges under and pushes up a warm air

mass, while a warm front rises up and over a cold air mass. When neither air mass has enough power to move into the area occupied by the other, a **stationary front** occurs. An **occluded front** is one in which a cold front overtakes a warm front. Prepare drawings similar to the diagram shown here to compare the movement of air masses in the four types of fronts.

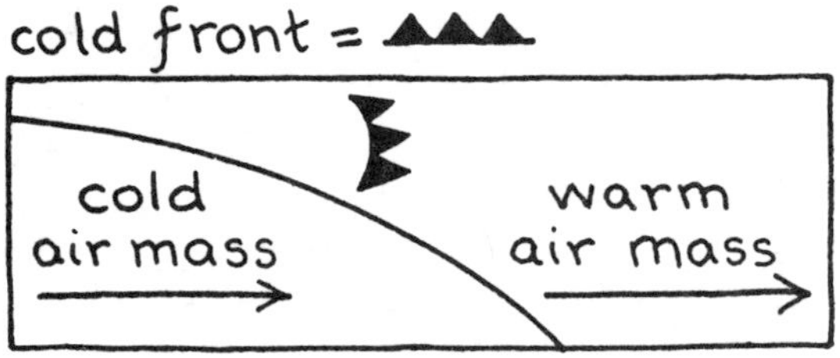

cold front = ▲▲▲

cold air mass →   warm air mass →

2a. Collect newspaper weather maps and watch a local media weather broadcast for one week to determine how fronts affect the weather from day to day. Make an enlarged drawing of a map and plot the most westerly cold front. Use pens of various colors to show the location of the front each day as it moves east. Use the maps to record the weather conditions, such as pressure, temperature, winds, and clouds before and after the front passes through an area.

b. Repeat the above procedure, plotting the movement of any of the other three types of fronts that are present during the week.

CHECK IT OUT!

1. The formation of warm and cold air masses occurs when air remains in a region long enough to take on the temperature and humidity of that region. Find out more about air masses. How long does it take an air mass to form? In what general direction do air masses move?

2. The weather before and after a front arrives can change subtly or very dramatically. Fronts are often part of larger weather systems. Find out more about the effect of fronts on the weather. What types of clouds are associated with each type of front? How do storms form?

 **10**

Cloud Maker

PROBLEM

How does a cloud form?

Materials

scissors
ruler
rubber glove (type used when washing dishes)
quart (liter) glass jar
tap water
match—to be handled only by an adult
two wide, medium-sized rubber bands
desk lamp
sheet of black construction paper
adult helper

Procedure

1. Cut a 5-inch (12.5-cm) square from the top of the glove.

2. Rinse the inside of the jar with water.

3. Pour most of the water out of the jar, leaving only enough to cover the bottom of the jar.

4. Ask an adult to light the match and allow it to burn for about three seconds. Then blow out the match and have your adult helper hold the smoking end inside the jar for two seconds.

5. Immediately stretch the rubber square over the mouth of the jar and ask your helper to place the rubber bands over the rubber square and around the neck of the jar. The rubber bands must be tight enough to hold the rubber square in place.

water

6. Turn the jar on its side and rotate it so that the water washes over the inside walls of the jar.

7. Hold the jar in front of the lamp so that the lamp illuminates the jar from behind and does not shine directly in your eyes.

8. Ask your helper to hold the sheet of black construction paper about 12 inches (30 cm) behind the lamp.

9. With your fingers push the center of the rubber square down into the jar about 1 inch (2.5 cm).

10. Observe the contents of the jar.

11. Pull the center of the rubber square upward about 1 inch (2.5 cm).

12. Observe the jar's contents with the rubber square stretched upward, and continue to observe as you release the rubber square.

Results

The contents of the jar look clear when the rubber square is pushed down. Pulling the rubber sheet upward causes the inside of the jar to become cloudy, but this cloudiness disappears when the rubber square is released.

Why?

When a liquid molecule acquires enough heat energy, it breaks away from the attraction of other molecules in the liquid and escapes as vapor into the space above the liquid. This process of changing a liquid into a vapor is called **evaporation**. Evaporation occurs faster if the surrounding temperature increases suddenly. **Condensation** (changing vapor into a liquid) is the reverse of this process, and it occurs faster when the surrounding temperature decreases suddenly.

In this experiment, when the rubber square is pushed into the jar, the increase in pressure causes an increase in temperature, thus more molecules of invisible water vapor are formed. When the rubber square is stretched upward, the contents of the jar expand, reducing the pressure inside the jar. The reduction in pressure causes a decrease in the temperature inside the jar, which in turn causes the water vapor to change back to water (a liquid).

These changes occur rapidly. When the rubber square is stretched upward, water molecules condense and cling to the smoke particles suspended in the air inside the jar, forming water droplets. These droplets are large enough to scatter the light, thus a **cloud** (a visible mass of water particles that float in the air, usually high above the earth) appears in the jar. The cloud scatters in various directions when the rubber square is released and the liquid water molecules evaporate. The tiny smoke particles are too small to scatter the light, so the jar appears clear.

LET'S EXPLORE

1. Does the number of smoke particles affect the results? Repeat the experiment twice. First ask an adult to hold the smoking match in the jar for five seconds; then do not add smoke to the jar.

2. Does the amount of water affect the results? Repeat the experiment twice.

First, do not place any water in the jar; then add ¼ cup (63 ml) of water. **Science Fair Hint:** Use separate jars for each experiment and display the jars along with diagrams representing the results of each experiment.

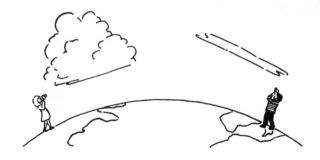

SHOW TIME!

1a. The three basic groups of clouds are cirrus, cumulus, and stratus. They were given Latin names by Luke Howard, a London pharmacist, in 1804. Use weather books, earth science texts, and/or encyclopedias to discover the description of the ten most common clouds: cirrus, cirrocumulus, cirrostratus, cumulus, cumulonimbus, altocumulus, stratocumulus, stratus, altostratus, and nimbostratus. Make a poster displaying these cloud types. Create diagrams, use copies of cloud pictures from books, and take photographs of clouds. Ask friends in different cities to assist in taking these photographs, since weather and clouds vary daily from one location to the next.

b. Prior to the development of modern instruments used to predict weather, meteorologists often accurately predicted the weather by observing clouds. Record a description of the weather and the type of clouds present each day for a week or more. Use your information to design a method of using clouds to forecast weather.

2. The upward motion of air, which causes a reduction in pressure and a decrease in temperature, produces clouds. Discover at what height each cloud type forms. Create and display a diagram showing low, medium, and high cloud types. One place you can find information on cloud types is on pages 50–52 of *The Weather Companion* by Gary Lockhart (New York: Wiley, 1988).

11

Rainy

PROBLEM

How do raindrops begin?

Materials

saucer
tap water
scissors
sheet of black construction paper
lid from a quart (liter) jar
petroleum jelly
table salt
desk lamp
magnifying lens
2-liter soda bottle with cap
timer
adult helper

Procedure

1. Place the saucer on a table. Pour enough water into the saucer to cover the bottom.

2. Cut a circle of black paper large enough to cover the inside of the lid. Place the circle in the lid.

3. Cover the paper with a thin layer of petroleum jelly. This will prevent the paper from absorbing water.

4. Carefully sprinkle salt grains on the paper in the lid. The grains should be kept separate from each other.

5. Hold the lid near a desk lamp. Use a magnifying lens to observe the salt grains.

6. Set the lid in the saucer of water.

7. Ask an adult to cut the bottom from the plastic soda bottle.

8. Secure the cap on the bottle and stand it in the saucer over the lid.

9. Lift the bottle and observe the salt grains through the magnifying lens

every 30 minutes for 3 hours. Observe the grains again after 24 hours.

Results

The grains are dry, white, and mostly cube-shaped before they are placed in the saucer of water. After 30 minutes in the saucer, the surface of the grains appears moist. As time passes, the grains look wetter, less white, and more transparent. Finally, no salt grains are present; only drops of liquid remain in the lid.

Why?

Rain droplets begin when water vapor condenses on tiny particles in the atmosphere, such as dust. These particles are called **condensation nuclei**. When such drops grow to a diameter greater than 0.02 inches (0.05 cm), they often fall as

rain. Rain is a form of precipitation (liquid or solid water particles that form in the atmosphere and then fall to the earth's surface). Nearly all precipitation begins as water vapor that condenses around small particles in the air.

This experiment demonstrates the condensation of water vapor on salt, a condensation nuclei that dissolves in the water. The liquid water in the saucer evaporated, as does water from the earth's surface. The water vapor inside the bottle was attracted to the salt grains because salt is **hygroscopic** (able to absorb water from the air). The water vapor condenses on the salt grains and the grains dissolve in the water, forming drops of salt water.

LET'S EXPLORE

Would drier air above the salt grains affect the results? Repeat the experiment placing the lid in a saucer without water. The result gives a clue to the formation of raindrops in areas of low humidity.

SHOW TIME!

1a. In the atmosphere, the condensation of water on small particles produces **cloud drops** (drops of water forming clouds with diameters between 0.00004 and 0.002 inches [0.0001 and 0.005 cm]) that are so small they remain suspended. The drops must grow before they become heavy enough to fall as raindrops. If the temperature in the cloud is above the freezing point of water (32 degrees Fahrenheit or 0 degrees Celsius), the growth of the drops occurs by **accretion**, which is the merging of water drops that bump into each other. Demonstrate how small water drops combine to form larger drops by covering a 4-inch (10-cm) square of cardboard with wax paper. The smooth side of the wax paper should be facing out. Secure the paper with tape and add

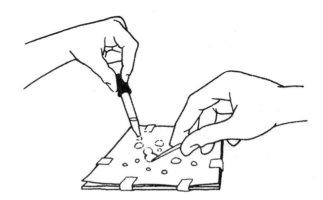

small drops of water. Use a toothpick to move the drops around so that they bounce into each other, and observe the results.

b. How big do the drops have to be before they fall? Prepare the drops as in the previous experiment. Quickly turn the cardboard upside down. Use the toothpick to move the small drops together until they become large enough to fall to the ground. While typical raindrops have a diameter of about 0.08 inches (0.2 cm), the falling drops from the wax paper will be larger because their weight must be great enough to overcome the attraction the water molecules have for the wax paper. Raindrops must be heavy enough to overcome the upward lift of air. Use photographs taken during this experiment to represent the results.

2. Make a poster comparing the size of cloud drops and raindrops. Show drawings of cloud drops and raindrops under a magnifying lens. Label the diameters of each.

3. How does an **updraft** (upward-moving air) affect raindrops? Inflate a 9-inch (23-cm) round balloon. Adjust a fan so that it blows upward, and turn it to high speed. Place the balloon over the fan. The force of the moving air holds the balloon in the air just as strong updrafts can support raindrops.

CHECK IT OUT!

Cloud seeding encourages tiny cloud drops to grow. Find out more about this method of modifying the weather. Information about cloud seeding, terminal velocity, and other cloud facts can be found on pages 72–78 of *The Weather Book*, by Jack Williams (New York: Vintage Books, 1992).

Dew Drops

PROBLEM

What causes dew?

Materials

two drinking glasses
tap water
ice
paper towel
timer

Procedure

1. Fill one of the glasses with water.

2. Fill the second glass with ice, then add enough water to cover the ice.

3. Dry the outside of each glass with the paper towel.

4. Allow the glasses to sit undisturbed for 15 minutes in an area without a draft.

5. Observe the outside of each glass.

Results

The outside of the glass of water without ice remains dry, but the outside of the glass of icy water is covered with water drops.

Why?

When air is completely filled with water vapor it is said to be **saturated**. Air may be saturated by adding water vapor, but since less water vapor is needed to saturate cold air, air may become saturated by cooling it. When air is saturated, condensation (the change of water vapor into a liquid) occurs.

The icy water cools the glass and the cold glass cools the air around it. Water vapor molecules in this chilled, saturated air clump together forming tiny drops of visible water. These droplets cling to the outside of the glass and grow as more water condenses on the glass. The glass containing water without ice does not cool the air enough for it to become saturated, and so the vapor in the air does not condense. Water droplets formed when water vapor in the air condenses on cool surfaces are called **dew**.

LET'S EXPLORE

1. Repeat the experiment using containers made of different materials such as glass, paper, and metal.

2a. The temperature at which dew forms is called the **dew point**. Determine the temperature at which the dew formed on the glass by repeating the original experiment using only the glass of icy water. Place a thermometer in the glass and watch the outside of the glass. Record the temperature when you first observe dew on the outside of the glass.

b. Does humidity (the amount of water vapor in the air) affect the dew point? Repeat the previous experiment on different days of varying humidity. Find out the humidity from the local weather reports in the newspaper or on television, and record it for each day the experiment is performed.

SHOW TIME!

1. Another way of testing how humidity affects the dew point temperature is to create a moist environment. Ask an adult to cut the bottom from a 2-liter soda bottle. Secure the cap on the bottle. Set the bottle in a saucer filled with water. Be sure the entire bottom edge of the bottle is below the water in the saucer. Allow the bottle to remain undisturbed overnight. The next day, lift the bottle and place a glass of icy water containing a thermometer in the saucer. Cover the glass with the bottle and observe the outside of the glass. Record the temperature at which the dew forms as in the previous experiments.

2. Determine changes in humidity by

constructing an instrument used to measure humidity called a **hygrometer**. Ask an adult to clean the oil from a 6-inch (15-cm) strand of straight hair. If you and your family members do not have straight hair, ask a friend or beautician for a strand. The adult can clean the hair strand by pulling it through two cotton balls moistened with fingernail-polish remover. Use a small piece of tape to secure one end of the strand of hair to the center of a toothpick. Color the pointed end of the toothpick with a marker. Tape the free end of the hair strand to the center of a pencil. Place the pencil across the mouth of a quart (liter) jar with the toothpick hanging inside the jar. If the toothpick does not hang horizontally, add a drop of glue to one end to balance the toothpick. Place the jar where it will not be disturbed. For a week or more, make daily observations of the direction in which the toothpick points. In moist air, the hair lengthens, and when the air is dry it shrinks. The stretching and shrinking of the hair pulls on the toothpick and causes it to move. From your results, determine how this hygrometer can be used to measure humidity. Repeat Let's Explore 2a. and b. to determine the effect of humidity on dew point, using this hygrometer to measure humidity.

CHECK IT OUT!

Dew does not fall from the sky like rain but forms on cooled surfaces. Find out more about dew. Why does dew usually form at night? How does the difference between daytime and nighttime temperature affect dew formation?

Frosty

PROBLEM

How does frost form?

Materials

7-ounce (210-ml) plastic glass
ice
tap water
paper towel
4 tablespoons (60 ml) rock salt (used
  to make homemade ice cream)
timer

Procedure

1. Fill the glass three-fourths full with ice.

2. Cover the ice with water.

3. Dry the outside of the glass with the paper towel.

4. Sprinkle the salt over the ice.

5. Gently shake the glass back and forth four or five times to mix the ice, water, and salt.

6. Scratch against the outside of the glass with your fingernail every 15 seconds for 2 minutes.

Results

A very thin layer of soft, white ice forms on the outside of the plastic glass, usually during the first 15 to 30 seconds. The frosty layer of ice is thicker after 2 minutes.

Why?

Frost is a light deposit of small, thin crystals of ice that form on cold objects when water vapor changes directly into a solid. Frost occurs when a layer of air comes in contact with a surface having a temperature below freezing (32 degrees Fahrenheit or 0 degrees Celsius). Salt lowers the temperature of the icy water below freezing, which cools the glass to a below-freezing temperature. Air touches the glass and, when this happens, the water vapor in the air changes directly into ice without first changing into water. The change from a gas directly to a solid without forming a liquid is called **sublimation**. Frost usually forms in nature when the nights are clear, cold, and calm and the air above the surface is relatively moist. Frost, like dew, is not precipitation because it does not fall from the sky, but forms directly on objects. The white color of the frost is due to air trapped inside the ice crystals.

LET'S EXPLORE

1. How much does humidity affect the formation of frost? Repeat the experiment on days of varying humidity. The local weather report in the newspaper or on television will give you daily humidity readings.

2. How much does wind speed affect the formation of frost? Repeat the original experiment four times. The first time, place the glass in a box where it will receive no wind. For the remaining trials, set the glass about 1 yard (1 m)

from a fan. First perform the experiment with the fan on low speed; then with the fan on medium; then with the fan on high speed.

3. At what temperature does the frost form? Repeat the original experiment placing a thermometer in the glass. Carefully add the ice, water, and salt. Record the temperature at which the frost begins to form.

4. Repeat the original experiment using containers made of different materials such as glass, paper, and metal. **Science Fair Hint:** The different containers and the results can be used as part of the display.

SHOW TIME!

1. Another way to produce frost is to place an empty drinking glass in a freezer for 15 minutes. Remove the glass and scratch the outside surface with your fingernail for evidence of frost formation. If no frost forms, repeat the experiment on days of varying humidity.

2. Does the temperature difference between air and the object it touches affect the formation of frost? Compare the effects of cold air touching a cold object and warm air touching a cold object by placing a small baby food jar inside a large, wide-mouthed jar. Secure the lid on the large jar and place it in the freezer. After 30 minutes take the jar out. Leave the lid

closed, and observe the surface of the two jars for 2 to 3 minutes. You can remove any frost that might form on the outside jar with a wet paper towel in order to observe the surface of the smaller jar inside.

3. Frost is not frozen dew. Prepare dew by filling a plastic glass with ice and covering the ice with water. Allow the glass to stand until large drops of water (dew) form on the outside. This should take about 5 to 10 minutes. Place the glass in a freezer. Remove after one hour and observe the frozen dew. Compare the appearance of frost made in previous experiments to the frozen dew.

CHECK IT OUT!

White frost is called hoarfrost. Hoarfrost forms when water vapor touches a very cold surface and freezes instantly, leaving long spiky needles. Hoarfrost usually occurs when the air is humid, the temperature of the air is around the freezing point (32 degrees Fahrenheit or 0 degrees Celsius), and the surface the air touches is significantly below the freezing point. Black frost occurs when the air is relatively dry and the temperature is below the freezing point. Find out more about frost. How is the intensity of frost determined? What is radiation frost? How is fern frost formed?

Icy

PROBLEM

How do icicles form?

Materials

straight pin
7-ounce (210-ml) paper cup
marking pen
masking tape
tap water
scissors
paper towel
5-ounce (150-ml) paper cup
sharpened pencil
index card
7-ounce (210-ml) clear plastic glass
timer
adult helper

Procedure

NOTE: You must have access to a freezer.

1. Ask an adult to make a tiny pin hole in the center of the bottom of the 7-ounce (210-ml) paper cup. Label this cup A.

2. Cover the hole on the bottom of the cup with a piece of tape.

3. Fill the cup three-fourths full with water.

4. Place the cup in the freezer.

5. Cut a circle from the paper towel the right size to fit in the bottom of the 5-ounce (150-ml) cup. Insert the paper circle into the bottom of the paper cup and label this cup B.

6. Hold cup B in one hand, and push the point of the pencil through the paper towel and out the bottom of the cup three times, to create three evenly spaced holes in the bottom of the cup. Some of the paper towel will hang down through the holes.

7. Cut a hole in the center of the index card just large enough so that cup B

fits into the hole with about 2 inches (5 cm) of the cup extending below the card.

8. Place the index card over the plastic glass and set cup B in the hole in the center of the card.

9. After 30 minutes, remove cup A from the freezer. The water inside cup A should be in liquid form except for a few crystals of ice.

10. Remove the tape from the bottom of cup A and place cup A inside cup B.

11. Place the stack of cups in the freezer for one hour.

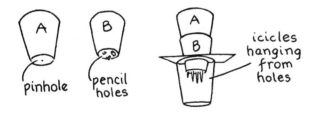

Results

A hanging mass of ice extends from each of the three holes in cup B.

Why?

The water in cup A is below its **freezing point** (the temperature at which a liquid changes to a solid), which for water is 32 degrees Fahrenheit (0 degrees Celsius). This **subcooled water** (liquid water below freezing point) is cold enough to **freeze** (change from a liquid to a solid), but at this temperature, ice crystals will not form without **freezing nuclei** (surfaces, such as dust particles or raised edges on rough surfaces, on which ice crystals can build). When the water drips out of the cup, some of its molecules stick to the fibers in the paper towel hanging from the holes. These water molecules provide a surface for other water molecules to attach to. Thus, ice crystals start to grow on the paper.

Gravity continues to pull the water drops in the cups downward. As a result, the dripping water moves down and freezes on the outside surface of the ice, forming an **icicle** (mass of hanging ice formed by the freezing of dripping water). Most of the water sticks to the top of the icicle, causing this section to be thicker than the end. The icicle grows longer as small amounts of water slide down and are slowly added to its entire length.

LET'S EXPLORE

1. How much do the hanging fibers in cup B affect the results? Repeat the experiment but cover only half of cup B with a piece of paper towel. Use the pencil to make two holes through the paper towel and the cup as before. In the side of the cup without the paper towel, make two holes by inserting the pencil point up through the bottom of the cup. **Science Fair Hint:** Display drawings of the results.

2. Do the sizes of the holes in cup B affect the results? Repeat the original experiment making holes of different sizes in the bottom of the cup.

3. Does the speed of the dripping water affect the results? Repeat the original experiment increasing the size of the hole in cup A. Use the point of the pencil to make the hole.

SHOW TIME!

1a. Winds play an important role in the melting of snow, ice, and icicles. Demonstrate this by placing two ice cubes of equal size in separate saucers. Place one saucer near a fan set on medium speed, and place the second saucer away from any air movement. Observe the ice cubes to determine which melts faster.

b. Determine the effect of wind speed on the melting of ice by repeating the previous experiment twice. First, do the experiment with the fan set on a low speed, and then do it again with the fan on high speed. Record and compare the melting time of the ice cubes at each wind speed. Prepare a bar graph to display the results.

2. The six-sided shape of snowflakes is due to the six-sided organization

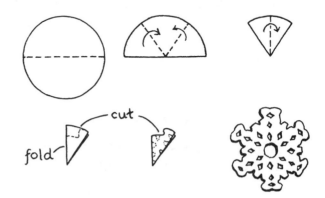

that water molecules assume when they freeze. Make a snowflake by drawing a circle on a sheet of unlined, white paper. Cut out the circle and fold it in half. Fold the half in thirds, and then fold that piece in half. Cut off part of the folded piece as shown in the diagram. Make cuts anywhere on the sides of the remaining piece.

Unfold the paper and you have a six-sided snowflake. This flake can be taped or hung with thread. Make different sizes of flakes by changing the size of the original circle. Use the paper snowflakes as part of your project display.

CHECK IT OUT!

Snow and ice are forms of frozen precipitation. Find out about other winter precipitation and frozen ice forms produced at frigid temperatures. What is sleet? Is sleet a universal name? What is freezing rain? How do graupel and ice pellets form? What is the difference between rime and glaze?

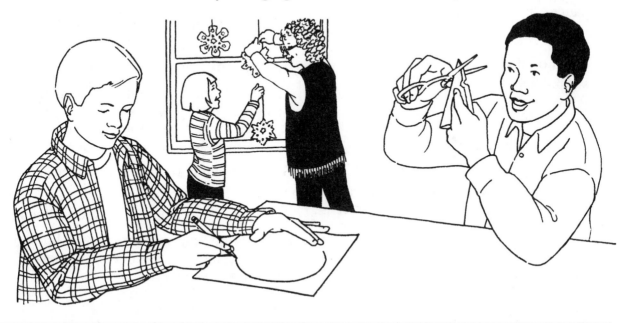

Layered

PROBLEM

How does hail form?

Materials

scissors
wax paper
saucer
eyedropper
cold tap water
sheet of black construction paper
desk lamp
paper towel
magnifying lens

Procedure

NOTE: You must have access to a freezer.

1. Cut a piece of wax paper to fit into the bottom of the saucer. Place the paper in the saucer.

2. Fill the eyedropper with water.

3. Squeeze about five drops of water

waxed paper
saucer

onto the wax paper spacing them apart from each other.

4. Place the saucer in the freezer.

5. After 30 minutes, remove the saucer. Fill the eyedropper with water and place one drop of water on top of each frozen drop.

6. Immediately replace the saucer in the freezer.

7. Repeat steps 5 and 6 two more times.

8. Wait one hour after the last addition of water, then remove one of the pellets from the saucer.

9. Place the black paper under the desk lamp and put the pellet on the paper.

10. Use the paper towel to dry the pellet, then turn it so that its flat side is facing up.

11. Use the magnifying lens to observe the structure of the ice. View it from different angles. Use the other pellets when the first one melts.

Results

The frozen pellet looks like a piece of ice that is rounded on one side and flat on the other. The surface of the flat side has a circular milky center with three rings of ice surrounding it. The rings in the pellets may vary; some are clear and some are milky looking.

Why?

Milky-looking ice is formed when water containing dissolved air bubbles freezes. If the air bubbles escape as the water freezes, clear ice is formed. As each drop is added, the clarity or cloudi-

ness of the ice produced depends on the amount of dissolved air bubbles that remain in the water as it freezes. **Hail**, like the pellets in this experiment, is formed by the addition of ice layers to a central piece of ice. Unlike the ice pellets in the experiment, hail is formed in thunderstorm updrafts. Sometimes water droplets in clouds are prevented from falling by strong updrafts of wind. These droplets are swept up into a cold cloud layer where they freeze and eventually fall when the wind can no longer support their weight. As these pellets of ice fall through warmer moist air, they become covered with raindrops. Another updraft sweeps the forming hailstones back into the upper, colder part of the cloud where subcooled water freezes on it. Snow may also stick to these

pellets, adding more layers and weight to the hailstones. As the hailstones move up and down in the cloud, they are covered by more and more layers of ice. When they finally become too heavy to be held up by the up currents of air, they fall to the ground.

LET'S EXPLORE

Does the temperature of the water drops affect the cloudiness of the ice layers that form the hailstones? Repeat the experiment twice. First, use water that you have chilled to 50 degrees Fahrenheit (10 degrees Celsius) by placing ice cubes in a cup of cold tap water. Repeat the experiment, using subcooled water. Prepare the subcooled water by filling a small metal food can with ice and then covering the ice with water. Set the can in a larger container, such as a coffee can or bowl that is as tall as the can. Fill the large container half full with ice and then sprinkle a layer of rock salt over the ice. *NOTE: Do not get salt inside the can.* Add a second layer of ice and rock salt to fill the container. Continue to add ice and salt to the larger container as needed throughout the

ground

experiment to keep the water subcooled. Use a thermometer to measure the temperature of the two containers of water.

SHOW TIME!

1. To show the individual layers in a hailstone, repeat the original experiment using water mixed with food coloring. Alternate layers of colored and uncolored water, or use different colors for each drop added. Display drawings of this experiment along with a summary of the results.

2. Grow a complete hailstone on a thread. Start the growing process by placing a piece of wax paper in a saucer. Lay the end of a 6-inch (15-cm) piece of thread in the center of the paper. Use an eyedropper to place one drop of water over the end of the thread. Place the saucer in the freezer. After one hour remove the thread and the piece of ice from the paper. Use tape to secure the free end of the thread to a pencil. Place the pencil across the mouth of a quart (liter) jar with the thread and the pellet of ice hanging inside the jar. Place the jar in the freezer. Prepare a cup of subcooled water as in the previous experiment. After 30 minutes, remove the jar from the freezer. With the pencil, lift the ice stone out of the jar and dip it into the subcooled water. Replace the pencil and the stone in the jar as before and return the jar to the freezer. Repeat this procedure three times. Photographs can be taken and displayed to show the change in the size of the simulated hailstone.

Flashers!

PROBLEM

What causes lightning?

Materials

duct tape
helper

Procedure

1. Unroll about 4 inches (5 cm) of the tape from the roll, but do not cut the strip of tape.

2. Hold the roll of tape in one hand and the end of the tape in the other hand.

3. Position the roll of tape so that you are looking at the place where the tape is being pulled from the roll.

4. Ask a helper to turn off the lights in the room. The best results will occur in a completely darkened room.

5. Jerk the end of the tape several times so that more tape is unrolled very quickly.

Results

Flashes of light appear across the area where the tape is pulled from the roll.

Why?

Matter is anything that takes up space and has weight. All matter is made of tiny units called atoms. An **atom** is the smallest part of an element that retains the properties of that element. Atoms are made of smaller units called protons and electrons. There are only two known types of **electric charges**, positive and negative. A **proton** has a positive electric charge and an **electron** has a negative electric charge. Protons are located in the center or **nucleus** of the atom, and electrons are located around the outside of the nucleus. Each atom usually has the same number of electrons and protons; however, electrons can become separated from atoms. A separation of charges occurs in this experiment when the tape is quickly jerked from the roll. The sticky part of the tape and the surface of the tape still attached to the roll are each left with an excess electric charge; one has an excess positive charge and the other has an excess negative charge. The buildup of excess electric charges in one place is called **static electricity**.

The law of electric charges states that unlike charges attract each other and like charges repel each other. Electrons are able to move from one material to the other. The attraction between the positive and negative charges causes the movement of electrons between the two charged surfaces. This movement is called **static discharge**, which is a transfer of static electricity. This static dis-

charge energizes the atoms of the gases in the air, causing a spark of light.

Lightning is just a larger flash of light due to static discharge in the atmosphere. Lightning occurs when charges separate within a cloud, making the bottom of the cloud more negatively charged than the top of the cloud. The negative charges in the bottom of the cloud repel the negative charges in the **neutral atoms** (atoms with the same number of positive and negative charges) in the ground or other structures directly beneath the cloud. Thus, the ground becomes positively charged because of the buildup of positive charges at the ground's surface. The electrons in the clouds move to the ground. This happens when the attraction between the negative charges in the cloud and the positive charges in the ground becomes great enough to overcome the air's resistance to electrical flow.

LET'S EXPLORE

1. Does it matter how quickly the tape is separated from the roll? Repeat the experiment twice. The first time, gently pull the tape off the roll. The second time, jerk the tape with more force than in the original experiment.

2. Would tape made from other materials affect the results? Repeat the original experiment using different kinds of tape, such as masking tape, electrical tape, and transparent tape.

SHOW TIME!

1a. Produce static discharge another way. Cut a 1-by-8-inch (2.5-by-20-cm) strip from a plastic report folder. Stand a paper clip upright in a piece

of clay on a table. Darken the room and then rub the plastic strip with a piece of wool cloth, such as a wool scarf. Immediately hold the plastic near, but not touching, the top of the paper clip. Look for the flash of light between the plastic and the clip. Display a drawing of the results along with a drawing of a lightning flash.

b. Can other materials be charged enough to produce a static discharge? Repeat the above experiment replacing the plastic strip with other materials, such as an inflated balloon, paper, aluminum foil, and cellophane.

CHECK IT OUT!

1. It is not fully understood how clouds become charged. One theory is that as strong winds toss raindrops around, the drops rub against each other and exchange electrons. The drops that gain electrons have a heavier, negative charge and fall to the bottom of the cloud. The drops that lose electrons have a lighter, positive charge and are swept to the top of the cloud. Use a chemistry or physics text to find out more about charged particles, or talk with a chemistry or physics teacher. Ask if the difference in the weight of a negatively charged drop and a positively charged drop is enough to cause the charge separation in clouds.

2. Find out more about lightning. What are the maximum volts of potential energy contained in a lightning stroke? To what temperature is the air around lightning heated? What causes the color of lightning?

Boom!

PROBLEM

What causes thunder?

Materials

9-inch (23-cm) round balloon
glove
straight pin

Procedure

1. Inflate the balloon to about half of its normal size, about 4 inches (10 cm), and make a knot.

2. Lay the inflated balloon on a table.

3. Place the glove on one hand.

4. Hold the pin with the gloved hand.

5. Stand at arm's length from the balloon.

6. Stick the pin into the balloon.

Results

When the pin is inserted into the balloon, the balloon rips. At the same time a loud popping noise is heard.

Why?

When your lungs force air inside the balloon, the rubber stretches and the balloon inflates. The air inside the balloon pushes outward. The stretched rubber pushes the air inside the balloon.

Sticking the pin into the balloon makes a tiny tear. The stretched rubber immediately starts to pull at the tear. At the same time, the compressed air rushes out and pushes on the tear. The balloon breaks apart.

As the compressed air rushes through the tear, it expands (moves apart). This quick expansion of air pushes outward

against the air surrounding the balloon. This creates sound waves that reach your ears as a popping sound. Thunder is produced in a similar way. As lightning strikes, it gives off energy that heats the air through which it passes. This heated air quickly expands, then cools and contracts. The fast expansion and contraction of air around lightning causes air molecules to move back and forth, which in turn produces sound waves that you hear as **thunder**.

LET'S EXPLORE

1. Does the amount of air in the balloon affect the results? Repeat the experiment twice; the first time, inflate the balloon to about 2 inches (5 cm); and the second time, inflate the balloon to its full size of about 9 inches (23 cm).

2. Does the shape of the balloon affect the results? Repeat the experiment using balloons of different shapes. **Science Fair Hint:** Inflate and photograph the different balloons used. Display the photographs along with the results of the experiments.

3. How does the content of the balloon affect the results? Repeat the original experiment. Fill the balloon with water by stretching the mouth of the balloon over an outside water faucet. Lay the balloon on a table outdoors. When the balloon is pricked, compare the sound made by the balloon filled with water to the sound of the balloon filled with air. When explaining any differences in the experiments, remember that water is much more difficult to compress than air.

SHOW TIME!

1. How does the speed of the expanding air affect the results? Inflate a 9-inch (23-cm) balloon to about half its normal size. Place a 1-inch (2.5-cm) piece of duct tape over a section near the neck of the balloon. Be sure the tape sticks smoothly to the balloon's surface. Put gloves on both hands. With one hand, hold the balloon at arm's length against a table. Stick the pin through the tape with the other hand. Remove the pin and allow the compressed air to slowly leak out. If the balloon breaks, as in the original experiment, the tape did not stick to the balloon. Try again.

2. There are other ways to show the fast expansion of air:

- Fill a sealable plastic bag with air and close it. Hold the bag in your hands and squeeze firmly until the bag opens.

- Fill a paper lunch bag by blowing into it. Twist the open end and hold it closed with one hand. Quickly and forcefully hit the bag with your free hand.

- Listen as you open a warm can of soda. The gases inside the can expand quickly when the can is opened, producing the fizzing sound you hear.

3. You can figure out how far away a lightning stroke is from you. Count the seconds from the instant you see the lightning until you hear the thunder. Divide the seconds by five to calculate the number of miles away the lightning was. For kilometer distances, divide the seconds by three.

CHECK IT OUT!

1. Lightning is a flash of light, and thunder is a booming sound. Why is thunder always heard *after* the lightning flash is seen? Find out about the speeds of light and sound. Does air temperature affect either one?

2. Often lightning flashes are seen but no thunder is heard. Find out how far from a flash of lightning the sound of thunder is carried. How would wind force and direction affect the distance? Is the type of lightning stroke a factor in this distance?

Twister

PROBLEM

What is the shape of a tornado?

Materials

two 2-liter clear plastic soda bottles
tap water
paper towel
flat, metal washer with the same
   circumference as the mouth of the
   bottles
duct tape
adult helper

Procedure

1. Ask your adult helper to remove the plastic rings left on the necks of the bottles when the lids are removed.

2. Fill one bottle half full with water.

3. Dry the mouth of the bottle with the paper towel and place the washer over the mouth of this bottle.

4. Place the second bottle upside down on top of the washer.

5. Secure the bottles together with tape.

6. Turn the bottles upside down so that the bottle with the water is on top. Stand the bottles on a table.

7. Place one hand around the lower bottle and the other hand on top of the upper bottle.

8. Support the lower bottle while quickly moving the top of the upper bottle in a small counterclockwise circle.

9. Stand the bottles upright, with the empty bottle remaining on the bottom.

washer

Results

The water inside the upper bottle swirls in a counterclockwise direction, forming a funnel shape as it pours into the lower bottle.

Why?

The funnel formed by the swirling water is called a **vortex** (a whirling mass of air or water). The vortex formed in the water is the same shape as the vortex formed by a **tornado** (a violently rotating funnel cloud that touches the ground). A tornado looks like a swirling funnel hanging down from a dark thundercloud. The swirling air that forms the funnel of a tornado appears to begin at the bottom of a dark, puffy, cumulonimbus cloud and moves down to the ground. Sometimes a funnel cloud simply dangles in the air and then seems to disappear or be drawn back into the cloud. The funnel can consist of winds spinning at speeds of more than 400 miles (640 km) per hour. The length of the funnel extending from the sky varies, but it may be 2,000 feet (615 m) or more. The diameter of the funnel's destructive tip varies from a few yards (meters) to a thousand or more yards (meters), with an average diameter of about 400 yards (400 m).

Condensed water vapor inside the swirling funnel gives tornadoes their gray color. When a funnel cloud nears and/or touches the ground, it acts like a giant vacuum cleaner. The condensed water vapor plus dust, soil, and debris it sucks up makes it appear blackish.

LET'S EXPLORE

1. Can the water swirl in the opposite direction? Repeat the experiment, rotating the bottle in a clockwise direction. Some scientists believe that tornadoes are set in motion by masses of air whose movements depend on the rotation of the earth. If this is true, all northern hemisphere tornadoes should spin in a counterclockwise direction and southern hemisphere tornadoes should spin clockwise. While that is usually the case, clockwise tornadoes have been seen in the northern hemisphere. **Science Fair Hint:** What do meteorologists think about the direction of the spin of tornadoes? Take a survey by asking

for the opinions of several meteorologists, such as those reporting the weather for a local television station or for the national weather forecasting stations on the radio. Call or write letters to get the information.

2. How does the energy applied to the bottles affect the results? Repeat the original experiment twice, first moving the bottle slowly and then moving it quickly. Compare the sizes of the funnels created in this experiment with

the one produced in the original experiment. **Science Fair Hint:** Display drawings of the results and compare them to information about the production of different sizes of tornadoes.

SHOW TIME!

1. Swift upper-level winds often make the top part of a tornado move forward faster than the lower part. That, in addition to friction that occurs where

the bottom of the funnel touches the ground, makes the lower part appear to drag behind. The funnel looks like a long, trailing rope or a snake dangling and wiggling from the sky. Demonstrate the difference in the forward movement of the top and bottom parts of the funnel. Hold one end of a string about 1 yard (1 m) long and pull it through the air. Repeat this movement, allowing the free end to touch the ground as you pull the top forward. Have a helper take photographs. Display photos of the string next to photos of tornadoes tilted at similar angles.

2. Tornadoes often perform freakish tricks. On June 23, 1944, a tornado passed over the West Fork River in West Virginia and drained it completely for a few minutes. Tornadoes are usually very destructive, yet fragile objects such as eggs and mirrors have been carried several miles by these violently whirling winds and lowered unharmed to the ground. Diagrams illustrating this and other odd events involving tornadoes can be used as part of a display.

CHECK IT OUT!

More tornadoes form on the flat central plains region east of the Rocky Mountains in the United States than anywhere else on the earth. Find out more about the formation of tornadoes. What weather conditions spawn tornadoes? Why do so many tornadoes form in the central plains region of the United States? Do tornadoes occur only in the United States?

Stormy

PROBLEM

What is the eye of a hurricane?

Materials

2-quart (2-liter) plastic bowl
tap water
scissors
string
ruler (the kind that has been punched
   for a three-ring binder)
paper clip
masking tape
black pepper
wooden spoon with a long handle

Procedure

1. Fill the plastic bowl three-fourths full with water.

2. Cut the string so that it is 1 inch (2.5 cm) longer than the height of the plastic bowl.

3. Tie one end of the string to the paper clip.

4. Thread about 1 inch (2.5 cm) of the free end of the string through the hole in the center of the ruler. Tape the end to the ruler.

5. Sprinkle pepper over the surface of the water in the bowl.

6. Stir the water with the spoon in a counterclockwise direction a few times.

7. While the water is swirling, quickly suspend the paper clip in the center of the swirling water. Try to drop the paper clip directly in the center of the spiral made by the swirling pepper specks.

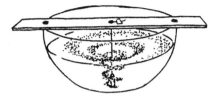

Results

As long as the paper clip remains in the exact center of the swirling water, it moves slightly or not at all.

Why?

The swirling water in the experiment represents a **hurricane**. A hurricane is a large tropical storm with winds of 74 miles (118 km) per hour or more that rotate around a relatively calm center. The center of the swirling water in this experiment simulates the calm area in the center of a hurricane called the eye of a hurricane. The eye is a long, vertical tube of relatively motionless air in the middle of the storm. The distance across the eye of a hurricane varies depending on the size of the storm, but it averages about 20 miles (32 km) across. This area of calm air reaches all the way to the earth's surface and has high-speed winds spinning around it. In the northern hemisphere a hurricane's winds spin counterclockwise around the eye, and in the southern hemisphere the winds spin clockwise. Like the air in a hurricane's eye, the area in the center of the swirling water in the bowl is relatively calm, as is indicated by the paper clip's lack of motion.

LET'S EXPLORE

1. How would suspending the paper clip near the side of the bowl affect the results? Repeat the experiment twice, first suspending the paper clip in the water on the side nearest to you, and then suspending the paper clip in the water on the side farthest from you.

Hurricane in Northern Hemisphere

Science Fair Hint: Use the results of this experiment to illustrate how the direction of the winds of a hurricane would change as it passed directly over you. Find out more about the weather conditions you would experience during a hurricane. A diagram illustrating the results can be used as part of a project display.

2. Does the size of the container affect the results? Repeat the experiment twice, first using a smaller bowl, and then using a larger bowl. **Science Fair Hint:** Find out more about the size of hurricane eyes. Does the size of the eye increase as the storm increases? Does the rotation speed of the storm affect the size of the hurricane's eye? Display drawings of hurricanes, comparing their size to the size of their eyes.

SHOW TIME!

1. Where is the rotation speed of swirling water the fastest? Fill a 2-quart (2-liter) bowl three-fourths full with water. Place a piece of tape on the top edge of the bowl. Cut two small triangles from a piece of notebook paper. Slowly stir the water in a circular motion. Drop one of the paper triangles near the center of the water. At the same time, ask a helper to drop

the second paper triangle in the water near, but not touching, the side of the bowl. Count the number of times that each piece of paper passes the tape in 10 seconds. (Hint: You should each keep track of one triangle.)

You should repeat this experiment at least three times and calculate the average number of rotations for each piece of paper. How do your results relate to the difference in the speed of winds of a hurricane near its eye and the speed of winds at its outer edges?

2. The official hurricane season for North Atlantic hurricanes is June 1 through November 30. Find out the dates for the hurricane season in your area, request a hurricane tracking map from your local media weather station, and plot the positions of hurricanes. For information about plotting the coordinates of a hurricane, see pages 116–123 of *Janice VanCleave's Geography for Every Kid* (New York: Wiley, 1993).

CHECK IT OUT!

1. Hurricanes occur on every continent except Antarctica. In Australia they are called *willy-willies*. Find out more about the different names given to hurricanes in various parts of the world. Make and display a map of the world showing hurricanes with their special names.

2. Hurricanes almost always begin over tropical seas during late summer and early fall. Moist air and heat are the two fuels needed to start and maintain these storms. Find out more about the birth and growth of these storms. What water-surface temperature is needed? What are the names of the different stages of development, and what is the wind speed of each stage? Which way do hurricanes move? What is their traveling speed? What is the average life span of hurricanes?

Indicators

PROBLEM

How do scientists gather clues to climates of the past?

Materials

modeling clay in three different colors
two index cards
1 teaspoon (5 ml) rice
straw
fingernail scissors
magnifying lens
adult helper

Procedure

1. Soften the clay by squeezing it in your hands. Break off a walnut-sized piece of each color of clay.

2. Flatten one of the clay pieces, and lay it in the center of one index card.

3. Sprinkle the rice over the top surface of the flattened clay piece.

4. Flatten the remaining two pieces of clay and stack them on top of the layer of rice. A three-layer block of clay about 1-inch (2.5-cm) deep will be formed.

5. Push the straw through the layers of clay.

6. Pull the straw out of the clay.

7. Ask an adult to use the scissors to cut open the straw.

8. Carefully remove the clay plug and lay it on the second index card.

9. Use the magnifying lens to study the clay plug.

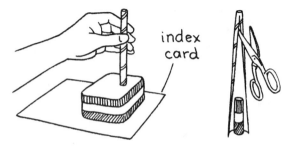

index card

Results

The straw cuts a cylinder-shaped sample from the layered stack of clay. Three layers of clay and possibly some rice can be seen.

Why?

As the straw cuts through the clay, the clay and rice are pushed up inside the hollow tube. The clay represents different layers of the earth's **crust** (thin outer layer of the earth), and the rice represents solids, such as **fossils** (traces of the remains of prehistoric animals and plants). The captured clay is called a **core sample**, and it reveals what materials are inside the block of clay. Machines that capture core samples are called coring devices. Made of metal, they are used to cut through layers of soil just as the straw cuts through the layers of clay. The metal coring device has a plunger that pushes the soil out so that materials at different depths below the earth's surface can be studied.

Scientists use core samples taken from ocean floors all over the world to discover important clues about the climate in past times. These samples contain tiny ocean creatures known as **foraminifera**, which are about one-fifth as wide as a human hair. These creatures have been preserved in the ocean floor for millions of years. The shells of these tiny ocean creatures have different shapes and makeups depending on the climate in which they were formed. These core samples from the ocean floor give scientists indications of the earth's major climate changes over the last 100 million years or so.

LET'S EXPLORE

1. Is the clay block exactly the same throughout? Repeat the experiment cutting core samples with the straw from different parts of the clay block. **Science Fair Hint:** Use diagrams to represent the size, shape, and color of each layer in the core samples.

2. The rice may not be visible on the outside of the core, but slices of the core sample can provide a better view of the core's content. Construct a saw to cut slices from the core sample by tying each end of a 4-inch (10-cm) sewing thread to toothpicks with rounded ends. Pull the toothpicks

SHOW TIME!

apart so that the thread is straight and taut between them. Place the thread on top of the core sample near one end. Move the toothpicks back and forth to saw a slice from the end of the clay. Use the magnifying lens to study the surface of the slice of clay.

Science Fair Hint: Display photographs of core samples and slices along with diagrams of the magnified surfaces of the samples.

1a. Trees can also give clues to the weather of the past. The growth rings of trees reveal good and bad growing seasons of past years. Contact your local parks department or a tree-trimming company and request a slice from a tree trunk or limb to be used as part of your science display. Find out more about the growth rings of trees. How do the rings indicate the age of the tree? What differences appear in growth rings during good and bad growing seasons? Display the tree slice, and label rings from these good and bad seasons. Note the age of the tree from which the slice was taken.

b. Examine the slice and use a pictograph similar to the diagram to represent the good and bad growing seasons during the life of the tree.

c. If possible, collect different tree slices and compare growth seasons during the same years. Prepare a pictograph of growing seasons for each tree slice.

d. If one is available, use a measuring instrument called calipers to more accurately determine the width of the growth rings in a cross section of a tree branch or trunk. Compare the width of each ring to the average rainfall and temperature during the year that the ring was formed. Ask a local media meteorologist for information about the average rainfall and temperature in the area where the tree grew.

CHECK IT OUT!

Core samples taken in ice layers contain bubbles of air. These tiny trapped air bubbles show which gases were present in the atmosphere when falling snow trapped the air. Find out more about other clues left by nature that reveal information about past climates. How are fossil plants, pollen, and animals used as past climate indicators? How do rocks give clues to the presence and size of glaciers?

Glossary

Accretion   Method by which a water drop grows as various water drops bump into each other and merge.

Air   Mixture of gases consisting of about 78 percent nitrogen, 21 percent oxygen, and 1 percent water vapor, carbon dioxide and other gases; Layer of gases surrounding the earth called the atmosphere.

Air mass   Large body of air with about the same temperature and humidity throughout.

Anemometer   Instrument that measures how fast the wind blows.

Atmosphere   Blanket of air surrounding the earth.

Atmospheric gases   Gases making up the layer of air surrounding the earth.

Atmospheric pressure   Force caused by the impact of moving air molecules on an area of the earth or any other object. Also called air pressure.

Atom   The smallest part of an element that retains the properties of the element.

Barometer   Instrument used to measure air pressure.

Calibrate   To determine and mark the position of individual measuring marks on an instrument such as a thermometer.

Carbon dioxide   Gas produced by burning fuels and exhaled by animals; part of the gases making up air.

Climate   The average weather in a region over a long period of time.

Cloud   A visible mass of water particles that float in the air, usually high above the earth.

Cloud drops   Drops of water forming clouds with diameters between 0.00004 to 0.002 inches (0.0001 and 0.005 cm).

Cold front   Leading edge of a cold air mass advancing into an area occupied by warmer air.

Condensation   Process by which a vapor changes into a liquid and requires a removal of heat energy.

Condensation nuclei   Small particles, such as dust particles, on which water vapor in the air condenses to form cloud drops.

Convection cell   A pattern of air circulation caused by unequal heating of the earth's surface.

Convection currents   Rising and sinking movement of water or air due to differences in temperature.

Core sample   A usually cylinder-shaped section cut from the earth's crust that reveals the materials at different depths.

Crust   Thin outer layer of the earth.

Current   Vertical movement of air.

Density   "Heaviness" of a material; Its mass compared to volume.

Dew   Water droplets formed when water vapor in the air condenses on cool surfaces.

Dew point   Temperature at which dew forms.

Electric charge   There are only two known types of electric charges, positive and negative. A proton has a positive charge, and an electron has a negative charge.

Electrons   Negatively charged particles located around the outside of the nucleus of atoms.

Equator   Imaginary line around the center of the earth.

Evaporation   Process by which addition of heat energy changes a liquid into a gas.

Foraminifera   Tiny ocean creatures with shells that differ in shape and makeup depending on the climate in which they were formed; give scientists clues to major climate changes over time.

Fossils   Traces of the remains of prehistoric animals and plants.

Freeze   To change from a liquid to a solid.

Freezing nuclei   Surfaces, such as dust particles or raised edges on rough surfaces, on which ice crystals can build.

Freezing point   Temperature at which a liquid changes to a solid; for water this temperature is 32 degrees Fahrenheit (0 degrees Celsius).

Front   Boundary between two air masses.

Frost   Light deposit of small thin crystals of ice on cold objects; formed when water vapor sublimes.

Greenhouse   Structure designed to provide a protected, controlled environment for raising plants indoors.

Greenhouse effect   Warming of a planet due to absorption and release of infrared waves by molecules in the atmosphere.

Hail   Layered pellet of ice formed in thunderstorm updrafts.

Heat   The total energy of all particles in an object.

Humidity   Amount of water vapor in the air.

Hurricane   A large tropical storm with winds of 74 miles (118 km) per hour or more that rotate around a relatively calm center called the "eye."

Hygrometer   Instrument used to measure humidity.

Hygroscopic   Able to absorb water from the air.

Icicle   Mass of hanging ice, formed by the freezing of dripping water.

Infrared waves   Heat rays; long wavelength energy waves such as those in solar radiation.

Kinetic energy   Energy of motion.

Light   A form of energy that travels in waves like water waves.

Lightning   Visible flash of light due to an atmospheric static discharge.

Matter   Anything that takes up space and has weight.

Meteorologist   Scientist who studies weather.

Meteorology   The study of weather.

Molecule   The smallest unit of a substance that still is that substance; two or more atoms linked together.

Neutral atom   Atom with the same number of positive and negative charges.

North pole   Area on the Earth that is farthest north from the equator.

Nucleus   Center part of an atom.

Occluded front   Front that occurs when a cold front overtakes a warm front.

Ozone   Form of oxygen containing three combined oxygen atoms, instead of two combined oxygen atoms like oxygen gas.

Ozone layer   Concentrated layer of ozone found between 10 and 20 miles (16 and 32 km) above the earth's surface.

Precipitation   Liquid or solid particles that form in the atmosphere and then fall to the earth's surface.

Protons   Positively charged particles found in the nucleus of atoms.

Rain   Water droplets with a diameter greater than 0.02 inches (0.05 cm) that form in the atmosphere and then fall to the Earth's surface.

Saturated   Completely full of fluid.

Seasons   Four periods of the year, each with specific weather conditions, called spring, summer, fall, and winter.

Solar radiation   Energy that is emitted by the sun.

South pole   Area on the earth that is farthest south from the equator.

Specific heat   Measure of the amount of heat needed to raise the temperature of one pound of substance one degree Fahrenheit (one gram of substance one degree Celsius).

Static discharge   Transfer of electrons between charged surfaces, which causes a spark of light.

Static electricity   Buildup of excess electric charges in one place.

Stationary front   Front that occurs when neither a cold nor a warm air mass has enough power to move into the area occupied by the other.

Subcooled water   Liquid water below the freezing point of water.

Sublimation   Change of a substance in a gas form directly into a solid without its forming a liquid, or the changing of a solid directly to vapor.

Temperature   Measurement in degrees of how hot or cold a material is; the average energy of motion of the molecules in a material.

Terrarium   Closed container housing small plants and sometimes small animals such as snails, frogs, or snakes.

Thermometer   Instrument used to measure temperature.

Thunder   Sound waves produced by the fast expansion and contraction of air molecules around lightning.

Tornado   A violently rotating funnel cloud that touches the ground.

Updrafts   Upward-moving air.

Visible spectrum   The rainbow colors—red, orange, yellow, green, blue, indigo, and violet. Each travels as light waves of different wavelengths.

Vortex   Funnel shape of a tornado. A whirling mass of air or water.

Warm front   Leading edge of a warm air mass moving into an area occupied by colder air.

Water vapor   Water in its gas form.

Wavelength   Distance from the top of one wave to the top of the next wave.

Weather   Condition of the atmosphere in a specific place at a particular time.

Weather vane   Instrument that shows wind direction.

Wind   Movement of air in a general horizontal direction; Winds move from high pressure to low pressure.

Index

air:
  composition of, 24–26
  definition of, 13
  saturated, 48
air mass:
  cold, 37, 38 39
  definition of, 37
  warm, 38, 39
air pressure, 12–15
anemometer:
  construction of, 32–35
  definition of, 34, 86
  Robinson, 34–35
atmosphere:
  air molecules, 9
  definition of, 5, 18
  gases of, 25
  layers of, 10–11
  temperature affected by, 24–27
atmospheric gases:
  composition of, 25–26
  definition of, 25
  ozone, 27
atmospheric pressure:
  definition of, 13
  wind production, 29–30
atom:
  definition of, 64
  neutral, 65
  parts of, 65
barometer, 12–15

climate:
  clues to past climates, 80–83
  definition of, 5
  sun's affect on, 4–7
cloud:
  cloud drops, 46, 47
  cumulonimbus, 73
  definition of, 42
  dissipation of, 42
  formation of, 40–43
  types of, 43
cloud drops, 46, 47
condensation, 42
condensation nuclei, 45
convection cell, 31
core sample, 80–82
currents, 28–31
  convection, 29
  definition of, 29
dew, 48–51
  definition of, 49
  dew point, 49
evaporation, 42
equator, 5
freezing nuclei, 57
frost, 52–55
  black, 55
  color of, 53
  definition of, 52
  hoarfrost, 55
front:
  cold, 38
  definition of, 38

  model of, 36–39
  occluded, 38, 39
  stationary, 38
  warm, 38
greenhouse effect:
  definition of, 26
  model of, 24–27
hail:
  color of, 61–62
  definition of, 62
  formation of, 60–63
heat, 22
humidity, 5
hurricane:
  birth of, 79
  definition of, 77
  eye of, 77
  models of, 76–79
  names of, 79
hygrometer:
  construction of, 50–51
  definition of, 50
icicles, 56–59
infrared waves, 25
law of electric charges, 65
light:
  color of, 9
  definition of, 9
  wavelengths of, 9
lightning:
  cause of, 65
  definition of, 65
  models of, 64–67

meteorologists, 18
meteorology, 18
North pole:
  definition of, 6
  sun's rays at, 6
precipitation:
  definition of, 5, 46
  rain, 44–47
  snowflakes, 58–59
rain:
  definition of, 46
  drops of, 44–47
raindrops:
  condensation nuclei, 45
  formation of, 44–47
  size of, 45, 47
  updraft affect on, 47
seasons, 6–7
sky:
  color of, 8–11
  weather predictor, 10
snowflakes, 58–59
solar radiation, 24–25
South pole:
  definition of, 6
  sun's rays at, 6
specific heat, 20–23
static electricity, 65
subcooled water:
  definition of, 57
  preparation of, 62
Sun:
  affect on climate, 4–7
  color of, 8–9

distance from earth, 10
light waves, 9–10, 11
radiation of, 24
ultraviolet light waves, 11
rays of, 4–7
sunrise, 9–10
sunset, 9–10
temperature, 17
terrarium, 27
thermometer:
  bottle, 18–19
  calibrate, 18
  definition of, 17
  Fahrenheit model, 16–18
  model of, 16–19
thunder:
  definition of, 69
  models of, 68–71
tornado:
  color of, 73
  definition of, 73
  freakish events, 75
  models of, 72–75
  shape of, 72–73
visible spectrum, 9
vortex, 73
weather:
  definition of, 5, 18
  sun's affect on, 5
weather vane:
  model of, 35
  definition of, 35
wind:
  cause of, 28–31

detector, 28–30
definition of, 29
speed of, 32–35

Get these fun and exciting books by Janice VanCleave
at your local bookstore, call toll-free 1-800-225-5945, or fill out the order form below and mail to:
Molly Chesney, John Wiley & Sons, Inc., 605 Third Ave., NY, NY 10158

Janice VanCleave's Science For Every Kid Series

___ Astronomy	53573-7	$11.95 US / 15.95 CAN
___ Biology	50381-9	$11.95 US / 15.95 CAN
___ Chemistry	62085-8	$11.95 US / 15.95 CAN
___ Dinosaurs	30812-9	$11.95 US / 15.95 CAN
___ Earth Science	53010-7	$11.95 US / 15.95 CAN
___ Ecology	10086-2	$11.95 US / 15.95 CAN
___ Geography	59842-9	$11.95 US / 15.95 CAN
___ Geometry	31141-3	$11.95 US / 15.95 CAN
___ Human Body	02408-2	$11.95 US / 15.95 CAN
___ Math	54265-2	$11.95 US / 15.95 CAN
___ Oceans	12453-2	$11.95 US / 15.95 CAN
___ Physics	52505-7	$11.95 US / 15.95 CAN

over 1 million VanCleave books sold

Janice VanCleave's Spectacular Science Projects

___ Animals	55052-3	$10.95 US / 12.95 CAN
___ Earthquakes	57107-5	$10.95 US / 12.95 CAN
___ Electricity	31010-7	$10.95 US / 12.95 CAN
___ Gravity	55050-7	$10.95 US / 12.95 CAN
___ Machines	57108-3	$10.95 US / 12.95 CAN
___ Magnets	57106-7	$10.95 US / 12.95 CAN
___ Microscopes & Magnifying Lenses	58956-X	$10.95 US / 12.95 CAN
___ Molecules	55054-X	$10.95 US / 12.95 CAN
___ Rocks and Minerals	10269-5	$10.95 US / 12.95 CAN
___ Volcanoes	30811-0	$10.95 US / 12.95 CAN
___ Weather	03231-X	$10.95 US / 12.95 CAN

Janice VanCleave's Science Bonanzas

___ 200 Gooey, Slippery, Slimy, Weird & Fun Experiments	57921-1	$12.95 US / 16.95 CAN
___ 201 Awesome, Magical, Bizarre & Incredible Experiments	31011-5	$12.95 US / 16.95 CAN
___ 202 Oozing, Bubbling, Dripping & Bouncing Experiments	14025-2	$12.95 US / 16.95 CAN

Janice VanCleave's A+ Projects

___ Biology	58628-5	$12.95 US / 17.95 CAN
___ Chemistry	58630-7	$12.95 US / 17.95 CAN

[   ] Check/Money order enclosed
(Wiley pays shipping. Please include $2.50 for handling charges.)
[ ] Charge my: [ ]VISA [ ]MASTERCARD [ ]AMEX [ ]DISCOVER
Card #:_____ Expiration Date:_____/_____
NAME:_____
ADDRESS:_____
CITY/STATE/ZIP:_____
SIGNATURE:_____
(Order not valid unless signed)

WILEY
Publishers Since 1807